The Afghan Syndrome

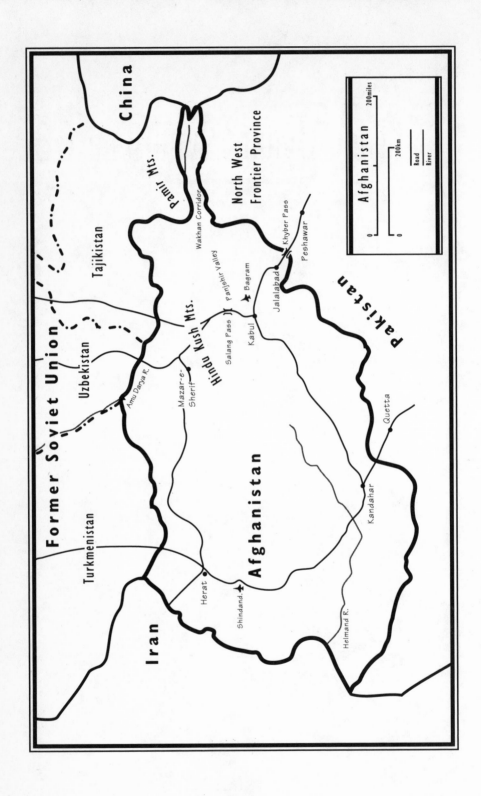

The Afghan Syndrome

The Soviet Union's Vietnam

Maj. Gen. Oleg Sarin
and
Col. Lev Dvoretsky

★

PRESIDIO

Published by Presidio Press
505 B San Marin Drive, Suite 300,
Novato, CA 94945-1340

Library of Congress Cataloging-in-Publication Data

Sarin. O. (Oleg Leonidovich)
The Afghan syndrome : the Soviet Union's Vietnam / Oleg Sarin, Lev Dvoretsky.
p. cm.
Includes index.
ISBN 0-89141-420-7
1. Afghanistan—History—Soviet occupation, 1979-1989.
I. Dvoretskii, L. S. (Lev Semenovich) II. Title.
DS371.2S27 1993
958.104'5—dc20   92-39125
                                                   CIP

Typography and map by ProImage
All photographs courtesy Oleg Sarin and Lev Dvoretsky
Printed in the United States of America

Contents

PUBLISHER'S INTRODUCTION

———

THE AFGHAN SYNDROME had its genesis, amazingly enough, from a totally unexpected source: Rotary International. Normally, Rotary as a service organization does not become involved in commercial business, particularly publishing. I was surprised, therefore, when a Rotarian friend, Frank O'Neill, called to ask if I would be interested in talking with a young Russian, Alexander Dvoretsky, then sitting in his office with some book ideas in his hand.

I responded affirmatively and later met with him. The result of this meeting was an invitation to the three members of Presidio Press attending the 1990 Frankfurt Book Fair to visit Moscow and discuss possible book projects with his father, the noted writer Lev Dvoretsky. October 1990 found us deep in negotiations with a group of extremely gracious and friendly people. Our talks resulted in our preparing together letters of intent to write and publish three books of recent Soviet military history, the first of which is *The Afghan Syndrome*. The principals in our negotiations were the authors, Maj. Gen. Oleg Sarin and Col. (Ret.) Lev Dvoretsky.

General Sarin was the deputy managing editor of *Red Star,* the daily newspaper of the Soviet armed forces. The paper has a huge circulation and is published in several daily editions to conform with the many time zones in their gigantic country. Oleg had a very large job, so I expressed a little wonder at his ability to devote enough time to write a complex book. He responded with a smile and the observation that he had "many talented helpers." Besides, he explained, his writing partner, Colonel Dvoretsky, being retired could bear a large portion of the research and writing load.

Several months passed after our return home before the first draft of the manuscript was sent to Presidio Press. It needed much work, so back it went to Moscow with many suggestions for rewrite. Again, several months later, the revised copy in English arrived and, still later, a large number of photographs. This did not mean smooth sailing, however, because the translation was evidently done by a team of linguists, all with different ideas on how to write the English language. What therefore began as a normal editing job resulted in a retranslation. We retyped it here, sent it to a sterling copy editor, Barbara Feller-Roth, and then submitted the "edited" manuscript to Oleg and Lev in Moscow.

Depending on their orientation, readers are going to have varied opinions of this book. Experts on the Soviet Union and Afghanistan are apt to find certain "facts" and conclusions with which they won't agree. They may conclude that certain sources are not reliable because they were part of the Soviet KGB disinformation campaign of those earlier days. I do not dispute this viewpoint, but instead argue that such information in a book like this is truly valuable because it shows a mindset in even enlightened scholars like Oleg and Lev caused by their entire orientation toward the Soviet governmental apparatus, in which they performed so ably. It may be more of a wonder that their writing is as objective as it is. I told them that I would not publish an apologia for Soviet actions in Afghanistan and I feel that they have met my demands. The book is admittedly not perfect, but does present for the first time in the West the war in Afghanistan through the eyes of two knowledgeable and patriotic members of the Russian armed forces. The reader will learn here of matters that were buried deep within the Kremlin archives. I think we owe Oleg and Lev our thanks for having unlocked some doors.

Robert V. Kane
Novato, California
November 1992

PREFACE

It was a warm spring day and dusk was falling over Washington. I realized I must get back to my hotel to pack, since I was returning to Moscow the next day. And yet, I couldn't tear myself away from the marble walls on which were inscribed many names and dates. It was the memorial to those who fell in the Vietnam War. I had always pictured that the memorial would look solemn and somewhat gloomy. I was right.

Not far from me an elderly woman was kneeling in front of the marble slabs. I felt I was intruding on her grief, but I couldn't move away. I was held by the expression of sorrow and pain on her face. They were the sorrow and pain of a whole nation. They also were my sorrow and pain.

With trembling hands the woman put a small piece of carefully folded paper into a slit between the two marble slabs. I thought it was probably a letter to someone who was no longer alive—her husband or son, or perhaps her brother. Her lips were moving silently. Was she praying? Perhaps she was saying something about those who were still living. Or was she condemning those who had sent him to his death?

Watching her, another picture came to me as if in a dream.

My recollection was of the Kuntsevo cemetery in Moscow. The leaves had turned yellow and a dreary drizzle was coming down. Another elderly gray haired woman was staring at the bright gold letters inscribed on a tombstone, as if unable to understand their meaning. "Died while fulfilling his international duty."

Yes, I remembered the scene very well. The woman was also whispering something, probably to her son, perhaps no more than nineteen years of age when he carried out his last duty inscribed on the tombstone as "international." That was not a duty he owed his mother or that she sent him to do. This nineteen-year-old lad didn't owe anything to anyone. Maybe she was telling him this. Or, perhaps she was condemning those who sent him away, made him believe that he was fulfilling some duty for his people, instead of merely serving the will of politicians who thought nothing of turning him into a victim in their nefarious game.

As I looked at the American woman mourning for some soldier who died in Vietnam, while recalling the Russian mother at the Kuntsevo cemetery, I realized that they both shared a common pain. It was then that the title for this book came to me: the Afghan Syndrome.

Much has been written and said about the Vietnam syndrome. For us, living in the Soviet Union during the Vietnam War era, it was nothing but a couple of words. We condemned that war and rejoiced in every successful operation by the guerrillas and at the ultimate defeat of American forces. Having been brought up in the spirit of internationalism, we were taught that the United States in those days was primarily an aggressor. We didn't stop to think what might lie behind the word *aggressor*. We didn't visualize the tragic fate of the thousands of people who had gone to that war in the belief that it was a just war, that it was their duty to take part in it. Misled and deceived by propaganda, they went to the recruiting center, moved by a feeling of patriotism. They had been assured that they would be fighting for a just cause. Months later, dying miserably in the tropical rain, they cursed those who sent them into the war, who had called it a "just war."

Finally, military action came to an end, but the war left its scars. It brought pain and suffering to hundreds of thousands of Americans and Vietnamese. The pain experienced by this generation will live on and be felt by the next generation.

The Vietnam syndrome—we weren't told anything about it; we weren't pained by it, but Americans were. Perhaps that was why it didn't occur to us that this disease was serious, that it could spread. Perhaps this was the reason why my country so thoughtlessly and rashly went to war in its own Vietnam.

For more than twelve years now the Soviet people have been pondering the war in Afghanistan. During this time we were able to analyze many of our thoughts about the war: from political indecisiveness at the beginning of the war to a clear realization of its horror; from feelings of patriotism riding high on a wave of internationalism to a Soviet documentary film entitled *This Was a Dirty War*; from dreamy falsehood to the harsh truth. This is our retrospective view of the Afghan war.

Years after the war was over, we see that our people and our generation walked the same road as the American generation of the 1960s. In 1980, Soviet mothers, like American mothers then, truly believed that their sons were fighting for a just cause. Our young people, like the young Americans then, volunteered for the front. We sincerely believed that the Afghans needed our help. As time went on and the props were removed, people began to see what really had been happening. American and Soviet mothers saw how civilians in Song-my and Kandahar died, killed by bullets fired by their sons. We, like the Americans earlier, began to ask ourselves: Who needed this war? Why was it called just? What did it bring to our people except pain and suffering?

Much has been written about the Afghan war, and more and more facts about the war have become known. We believe that this book will acquaint the reader with some episodes connected with the history of the war that have not been previously disclosed and will throw some light on the real aims pursued by Soviet political and military leaders in deciding to go to war in Afghanistan. We hope that the reader will find in this book a fresh and fair assessment of the war. But above all we have endeavored to show how the Afghan war has affected the Soviet people, especially the lives of those who have returned from the war to try to find their places in Soviet society today. Such an emphasis is not accidental. For a new generation of Soviet people has appeared: the "Afgantsi," Soviet soldiers who served in Afghanistan. A new attitude has arisen among our people, which we call the "Afghan syndrome." Its impact is being felt increasingly today as democratic reform (*perestroika*) changes our country.

Perestroika might have happened if there had been no Afghan war. But the Afghan tragedy made perestroika inevitable. Our return to universal humane values and ideas was by way of this war. Mikhail Gorbachev has assured the world that we have once and for all removed the subject of war and revolution from our consciousness and political doctrine. Such a statement is due in part to the bitter lesson of the Afghan experience. Because of Afghanistan, we have been able to surmount another psychological barrier and find the courage to admit that our military interventions in Hungary in 1956 and Czechoslovakia in 1968 were mistakes, that there could be no moral or political justification for our attempts to reshape the destiny of other nations. Our new understanding of internationalism, Gorbachev has pointed out, is linked to our affirmation of universal human values. Thus, our call for democratization of our country rests on an understanding that authoritarianism had led to the blind alleys of the Afghan war. When we say we must help the Afgantsi, we are thinking of more than moral and material recompense to those veterans. Society owes them something else: It owes them a debt of gratitude. It was they who helped the rest of us overcome ourselves, our inertness, our mistakes; it was they who helped stir our consciences.

The Afghan syndrome signifies not only our repentance, our wish not to repeat past mistakes or commit new ones, but our wish to live in conformity with normal laws of a civilized nation. Sadly, it is also a curse, a monster that still resides among us. It rears its head again and again when the demands of the moment seem more important than the real interests of people; when political expediency takes the upper hand over truth; when the fist becomes the sole argument and only brute force is believed capable of establishing justice. The parallels are evident: Baku and Nagorno-Karabakh, Tbilisi and South Ossetia, Lithuania and Moldova—Soviet cities and republics where troops have been used to restore order. The country's crime rate is rising; there is demoralization in the army.*

---

*According to official sources, there have been cases of desertion in some units of the Soviet Army and of young men refusing to be drafted. Cases where young conscripts were beaten up by senior officers have also been reported. In some republics— Lithuania, Latvia, Estonia, Georgia, Azerbaijan, and others—resolutions have been passed on setting up military units with their "own" conscripts.

Is not the blitz attack by Saddam Hussein on defenseless Kuwait an attempt to pursue our old logic that the strong can do anything they wish?

Some day our moral discoveries will lose their novelty; some day the new achievements of the human spirit will take their proper place. We should not be disheartened or saddened by such a prospect. On the contrary, we should rejoice when what we regard with pride today as the summit of common sense and humanism becomes something quite ordinary and natural. What we think and evaluate anew today will become, at last, accepted standards of life for all of us. We will no longer spend time debating and seeking new ways of solving problems that torment us today. The answers and solutions will come to us naturally, for they will have become part of our inner selves. For this to happen we must do all that is necessary today; we must experience and remember everything. Again and again we must tread the stones with which our road to Afghanistan was paved.

Chapter 1

FROM MONARCHY TO REPUBLIC

The Soviet military invasion of Afghanistan (1979–1989) came out of the blue, not only for the world community but also for the Soviet people. The news of the invasion was in sharp contrast to numerous declarations, acts, and announcements by Soviet officials during the preceding years of Soviet-Afghan relations. Then, the policy of noninterference and of friendship and cooperation with this neighboring country had been solemnly underlined.

The fact is that Afghan history is the story of nonstop internal conflicts among tribes, groupings, and national formations, both of the government and the opposition, as well as under the rule of the emir, between him and his opponents. The tzarist government of Russia, and later the Soviet leadership, have always tried to have a friendly neighbor in Afghanistan. In the past, Russian authorities never allowed themselves to influence the people and government of Afghanistan from a position of force, let alone to interfere overtly in internal affairs. It was quite obvious that any other approach was absolutely unacceptable and unprofitable. Such an approach to dealing with this small state had no future. Afghanistan was unique from the viewpoint of geography, national and linguistic variety of the population, social and state organization, and, most importantly, the love of its people for freedom. Many years ago, the long British military campaign against Afghanistan demonstrated clearly these unique characteristics of the Afghan people. So, a partner-like Soviet-Afghan relationship was apparent to the Kremlin, backed by both Soviet and western studies of Afghanistan.

Afghanistan has a rich history. It is believed that some parts of it were inhabited as long ago as the Stone Age, though the very name of Afghanistan dates back only to the thirteenth century. At that time it was an ethnogeographic entity including the area of the Suleiman Mountains, and regions to the south of them, to the Indus River. This is where the Afghans lived.

The unification of Afghans and the creation of an independent state came after the long fight against the rule of the great Moghuls and Safavids, who had dominated Afghanistan in the sixteenth century. The creation of the Afghan state happened finally in 1747 after Iranian Shah Nadir's death and the collapse of his empire. In October of that year in Nadirabad (near Kandahar) at a *jirga,* a meeting of representatives of different regions of the country, Ahmad Khan was elected the shah of Afghanistan, assuming the name of Ahmad Shah.

The first centralized Afghan state is also known as the Durrani empire. In the years of his rule (1747-1773), Ahmad Shah waged war frequently against his neighbors, expanding the borders of his state.

Later when his successors were in power, centralized rule in the country was significantly weakened by rebellions of non-Afghans living within the country. In 1818 the Durrani empire collapsed and princi-palities were formed: Herat, Kandahar, Kabul, and Peshawar.

Kabul later became the center of a new reunification of Afghani-stan, which was begun by Dost Muhammed (1826–1863). This nationalistic political movement coincided with the first Anglo-Afghan war (1838–1842), which ended with the catastrophic defeat of the British. Out of 16,500 troops and support units that were forced to leave Kabul on January 6, 1842, only one man made it to Jalalabad by January 13. It was he who brought the news of British losses in the disastrous combat with the Afghans.

The second Anglo-Afghan war lasted from 1878 to 1880. Once again the British were beaten. But seeing the damage and assessing the danger that any further war escalation might cause his country, the emir of Afghanistan made certain concessions to the British. Among other things, he agreed to conduct all diplomatic intercourse with other states through the British viceroy in India. This arrangement was acknowledged by all nations, including tzarist Russia. In accordance with the Anglo-Russian agreement of August 31, 1907, Russia agreed to use the British government as mediator in its political relations with Afghanistan.

Afghanistan was at this time an underdeveloped agrarian state. The wars with Great Britain caused immense material damage, negatively influenced the development of production, and limited the normal process of assimilating the Afghan economy into the world economic system. Only at the end of the nineteenth century did major Afghan landowners and merchants appear who were able to develop connections with world markets. They were able to quickly accumulate money and thus get high profits from their commerce. At the same time, trade in general was mainly with British India, so national capital played only a small role.

More than 90 percent of the population was made up of peasants and nomad herdsmen. The Pushtuns, despite taking up some farming, remained mostly nomads and cattle breeders. Other nationalities in Afghanistan, such as Turkomen and Uzbeks, who lived in the north, were also herdsmen, but of sheep and goats. Farming increased in importance in modern Afghanistan, mainly in the regions where the Tadzhiks and Hazaras lived. But farming was less prevalent than cattle breeding. Elements of a communal-tribal system were present, and slavery was not unknown. These elements of feudalism hindered the creation of a unified national market, and the multiethnic variety of the population and the great number of nomadic tribes made ruling the country difficult.

Except for small workshops, there was almost no industry in Kabul, so almost everything was imported. There were no railroads or other highways in the country. The main means of transportation of goods were caravans of camels, widely used internally. Only at the start of the century were secular schools opened. The Afghan economy at that time was greatly dependent on trade with other countries, especially Great Britain, facilitating the strengthening of British influence in the country.

Afghanistan was an absolute monarchy. The emir, Habibullah Khan, who headed the country since 1901, was referred to in English literature as an "indocile vassal," with good reason. For example, in his inauguration speech Habibullah Khan promised to conform to a policy of national unity, with needed reforms and resistance to aggression. He did not accept British proposals of new trade agreements, which he thought would make his country even more dependent on them. A British trade and diplomatic mission was sent to Kabul in 1904, but with no success. Only agreements acknowledging former obligations of Afghanistan to Britain were signed. Emir Habibullah Khan also refused to recognize the British-Russian agreement of 1907 as contradictory to the interests of his kingdom.

The obvious dependence on Great Britain and the suppression of any opposition inside the country caused a great amount of dissatisfaction in the majority of young Afghans who had been educated abroad, as well as military officers, liberal landowners, and public servants. These are known in history as Mlado-Afghans ("young Afghans"), who strove for restoration of full independence of the state, putting limits to the emir's authority, drafting a constitution, and implementing reforms that would ensure more favorable conditions for the development of the country.

The ideologist of this Mlado-Afghans movement was Mahmud Tarzi, the editor of the country's only newspaper, *Seraj Al Akhbar*. Tarzi was especially interested in developing industry and culture. But the Mlado-Afghans were repressed, their leaders thrown in jails and many of them executed.

The movement was influenced by the Russian bourgeois-democratic revolution of 1905-1907 as well as the national-liberation movement in India. In February 1916, young Afghans, together with Indian revolutionaries, sent a letter to Russian Tzar Nicholas II asking for help in their struggle against the English. The tzarist government did not respond to this appeal, but instead immediately informed British authorities of its contents. They in turn gave the information to the emir. The result was a new wave of repression.

The second bourgeois-democratic revolution in Russia in February 1917, resulting in the overthrow of the tzar, gave Afghan revolutionaries hope for help and support. So again, together with Indian revolutionaries, they sent a new letter on May 6, 1917, to Russia's capital with the same request for support in the struggle against the British. But this time also, the "Provisional Russian" government rejected the request.

A strange development was that Emir Habibullah Khan's son,

Amanullah Khan, became part of the Young-Afghan movement. His ideas were formed to a great extent under the influence of the members of the movement, but a more compelling reason may have been that Amanullah Khan was married to the daughter of Mahmud Tarzi.

Opposed to Emir Habibullah also were the so-called Old-Afghans, whose leader was Emir Habibullah's brother, Nasrullah Khan. This group represented right-wing reactionary factions including Moslem clerics and feudal elements. They dreamed of returning to old times and previous rules, restoring medieval orders that would guarantee privileges for them. Both Old-Afghans and Young-Afghans called for a military struggle against Britain, but the final goal of the Old Afghans was to strengthen their own position and isolate the country not only from the influence of Great Britain but the rest of the world as well.

The socialist revolution in Russia in October 1917 changed the attitude of Russia to Afghanistan. Steps were taken with the aim of establishing diplomatic ties. In June 1918, the chief of staff and chairman of the Soviet city of Kushka, Konstantin Slivitsky, who knew the Afghan language well, was sent to Kabul. En route he met in Herat with various local authorities, explaining the goals of his trip to them.

Emir Habibullah and his close advisors did not show much interest in establishing direct Soviet-Afghan relations. At that time Habibullah Khan actively supported the emir of Bukhara in his struggle against Soviet Russia, sending to Bukhara Afghan soldiers and English weapons.

At the end of 1918, Soviet Russia made another attempt to establish contact with the Afghan government. A letter was written to the Afghan emir that was to be taken to Kabul by Ibrahim Khan, the son of Afghan Prince Ishaq Khan,* who had lived in Samarkand for twenty years as an emigrant. The letter stated that Ibrahim Khan's trip was seen to be a "happy opportunity not only to stress our sincere good-neighbor sentiments but also our wish to develop friendly relations for the benefit of both our peoples." This attempt also failed. The Afghan emir denied an entrance visa to Ibrahim Khan.

This was due not only to the emir's negative attitude toward revo-

*Ishaq Khan, who was Emir Abdorrahman's cousin, since 1880 was the ruler of Mazar-i-Sharif. He tried to usurp power in Kabul but failed; his troops were defeated in September 1888. Ishaq Khan together with his advisors escaped. He was granted shelter in Samarkand.

lutionary changes in Russia, but also to the fact that by summer 1918 British troops had entered Iran and Trans-Caucasia and later Soviet Turkestan. Afghanistan thus found itself surrounded by British troops— in the southeast from India and in the northwest from Persia and Turkestan. In the event of war, this presented Afghanistan with the menace of being invaded from three sides.

Young-Afghans were definitely against the strengthening of British positions in Soviet Central Asia. They openly expressed their dissatisfaction with the emir's policy, which tended to favor military actions of Great Britain. The situation in the interior of the country also worsened. Many letters addressed to Habibullah called upon him to change his unpopular policies that were damaging the state and instead to pursue an independent sovereign policy in the interests of the Afghan people. A strong sign of deep dissatisfaction was the attempted murder of Habibullah in mid-1918. When the assassination attempt failed, more repressions occurred, which made the situation even more tense. Despite extreme precautions, on December 1, 1918, Habibullah and his court moved to Jalalabad, his winter capital. Conditions continued to ferment until the night of February 20, 1919, when Habibullah Khan was found murdered near Jalalabad where he was hunting.

The Old Afghans' leader, Nasrullah Khan, the old emir's brother, was in Jalalabad at the same time and proclaimed himself emir. Simultaneously, Amanullah Khan, the governor of Kabul, did the same there; he appeared before the regiments of the Kabul garrison, unsheathed his saber, and announced that he would not put it aside until Afghanistan was truly independent. Therefore, there were two authorities in the country between February 21 and 28, 1919.

But in Jalalabad, patriotic young officers seized power. They arrested ministers, feudals, and officers supporting Nasrullah. Several days later, when Amanullah Khan arrived from Kabul, they turned their support to him. The struggle for the Afghan throne was finally decided in favor of Mlado-Afghans.

Amanullah Khan's first act as emir was to declare Afghanistan a nation fully independent both in external and internal affairs. In his inauguration speech on February 28, 1919, he stated that from that time Afghanistan would not accept any foreign intervention. The new emir made the point that his government was independent and had all the rights and position of other sovereign states in the world.

As part of this new sovereignty, the emir announced that he did not consider himself required to abide by the treaties and agreements imposed on Afghanistan during the period of the former emir's rule.

On April 13, 1919, Amanullah Khan, speaking in Kabul, said: "I declare myself and my country fully free, self-managing and sovereign in all internal and external affairs. Thus my country will be a sovereign state as other states and empires of the world." Turning then to a British diplomatic agent, the emir asked him: "Did you understand what I said?" The agent answered: "Yes, I understand."[1]

Two days later, on April 15, 1919, a month and a half after the restoration of the complete independence of Afghanistan, British Viceroy of India Chelmsford demanded that Amanullah Khan must fulfill all obligations prescribed by former agreements. Britain did not acknowledge Afghanistan's independence. We believe this occurred because Britain saw the danger of losing her influence in this country, with its growing affinity to Soviet Russia. The British government decided to resort to stringent methods, including military intervention, to preserve its influence in Central Asia. On May 6, 1919, England officially declared war on Afghanistan. An army of 340,000 men with artillery, machine guns, mechanized units, aviation, and 185,000 horses and camels was concentrated near the Afghan border.

Confronting this strong force were 38,000 Afghan soldiers and 8,000 cavalry. The combat readiness of the Afghan army was low. They lacked combat equipment, and communications were practically nonexistent. Different units of the army had to act, not knowing anything about one another. But morale was high. An English official paper read as follows: "It is impossible not to admire the boldness with which they [Afghans] fought until the bitter end, not even thinking of surrender, though the simplest thing for them to do was to flee to Kandahar. . . ."[2]

The English historian A. Swinson estimates that the third Anglo-Afghan war was ". . . one of the most difficult campaigns on the border for the whole century of British rule there."[3]

The outcome of the war was greatly influenced by Pushtun participation in it. Their armed rebellion covered the entire border from Chitral in the north to Quetta in the south. Pushtun units ambushed Anglo-Indian regiments heading for Afghanistan and closed roads on them, hampering the advance of British headquarters and troops. As a result, the British command was not able to use all its forces. These bitter lessons of British military actions in Afghanistan unfortunately were neglected by Soviet leadership, which in 1979 decided to interfere in the domestic affairs of this country by military means.

In May 1919 Emir Amanullah Khan suggested peace talks under the condition that Britain acknowledge complete independence of Afghanistan. He said that if England sought to preserve the old status of Afghanistan, Afghanistan had no other recourse but to continue the war. Britain agreed and on June 3, 1919, an armistice was signed.

Between July 26 and August 8, 1919, in Rawalpindi, India, Anglo-Afghan talks took place, ended by the signing of a preliminary peace treaty.

The Soviet government immediately recognized Afghan independence and sovereignty. At the same time, all treaties and accords infringing on the interests of Afghanistan signed by the tzar, including the 1907 British-Russian agreement, were annulled. These steps cleared the way toward establishing diplomatic ties between the two countries.

On March 11, 1919, the chairman of Sovnarcom, V. Lenin, held talks with an American State Department spokesman, the attaché at the Paris Peace Conference, William Bullitt. American President Woodrow Wilson and British Prime Minister David Lloyd George sent representatives to Moscow to discuss a postwar settlement. The parties agreed that a draft treaty on Afghanistan should guarantee the joint obligation by the participants of the conference not to use force to overthrow the Afghan government. Soviet Russia together with other participants of the Paris Peace Conference signed a memorandum that emphasized the renunciation of the use of force by all the states against governments of smaller countries.

Amanullah Khan sent Lenin a letter announcing his coming to the throne and urgently proclaiming

. . . unity and friendship for the sake of peace and prosperity of mankind. As you, your majesty, my great and kind friend, president of the great Russian state, together with your comrades and friends of mankind, assumed the honorable and noble task of promoting peace and well-being of the people and proclaimed liberty and equal rights for the countries and peoples all over the world, I am happy to direct to you this message of good will on behalf of independent and free Afghanistan.[4]

On May 27, 1919, Lenin sent a letter to Kabul addressed to Amanullah Khan in which he welcomed the intentions of the Afghan government to establish friendly relations with the Russian people and suggested exchanging diplomatic missions.

> Having received the good-will message from the free and independent Afghan people with regard to the Russian people and the news of Your Majesty's coming to the throne, the government of workers and peasants and all the Russian people lose no time in returning our regards to the sovereign Afghan nation, heroically upholding its liberty. . . .[5]

The exchange of these letters actually meant mutual recognition of Lenin's government and Afghanistan and an agreement to establish diplomatic ties. The People's Commissariat on Foreign Affairs in a special note informed the Afghan Foreign Ministry of the fact that ". . . the Soviet government has scrapped all the secret agreements which were forced on smaller nations by powerful neighbors, including those of the tzarist government." The note emphasized that ". . . the Soviet government, as soon as it learned of the declaration of independence of the Afghan people, solemnly recognized Afghan sovereignty and supported its liberation struggle."[6]

Nicolay Bravin was delegated to Kabul to represent the Soviet government. Bravin (1881–1919) was the first Soviet diplomatic representative in Iran, then in Afghanistan. He was the only tzarist diplomat in Iran who welcomed the socialist revolution of 1917, agreeing to represent the Soviet government in Teheran. In the summer of 1918 Iranian authorities insisted that Bravin should leave Iran. Bravin's mission left Tashkent for Kabul in May 1919. But it proved difficult to reach Kabul. On its way to the Afghan capital the mission was attacked by armed tribes. Two members of the delegation were killed and eighteen wounded in the fighting. Despite this interference, the mission managed to cross the Amu-Darya River. The newspaper *Izvestya* reported on July 5, 1919, that the official representative of the People's Commissariat on Foreign Affairs had arrived in independent Afghanistan. Amanullah Khan ordered local authorities to welcome the mission and escort it with honor to Kabul.

On his arrival in the Afghan capital, Bravin informed the emir of the Soviet government's readiness to provide Afghanistan all kinds of assistance, including a supply of weapons. As a result of Bravin's visit and friendly attitude, late in September 1919, an extraordinary Afghan diplomatic mission left Kabul for Moscow to inform the Soviet government formally of the declaration of independence by Afghanistan as well as preparations to exchange permanent diplomatic representatives between the two countries. The Afghan ambassador, Gen. Muhammed Wali Khan, headed the mission.

High-level talks, including those with Lenin's participation, provided the foundation for Soviet Russia's ties with Afghanistan. After visiting Russia, the Afghan diplomatic mission intended to tour Europe and then the United States. The Soviet government, at the request of the Afghan mission, approached the representatives of various European nations to request security for the Afghans and arrange meetings for the Afghan diplomats. But not all European countries, as well as the United States, were ready to recognize the new independent Afghanistan at that time. So, the Soviet initiative failed to find any backing.

A process of dramatic reforms got under way in the early 1920s in Afghanistan. The reforms were aimed at eliminating the most archaic forms of the old regime and opening new paths for economic development. A series of practical steps undertaken by the Amanullah Khan government called for legal privatization of land, reforms in the tax system, and the abolition of slavery and slave trading still existing in certain parts of the country. The new government sought to encourage industry and to build the first improved roads in the country.

In 1922 the former emir's chief subordinates, advocates of the old regime who supported the archaic legal proceedings of the Middle Ages, such as quartering, hanging, and other draconian measures, were deposed. Amanullah Khan's close associates and ministers were assigned to the provinces where they declared equality of all before the law. Bribery, corruption, and all kinds of graft as well as barbaric punishments were strictly prohibited.

Much was accomplished in educating the people. An academy for girls and a number of other civil schools were opened in Kabul. Medical service was gradually improved by doctors with European educations.

There were changes in Afghan foreign policy also, especially a more friendly attitude toward Soviet Russia. In Kabul on September 13, 1920, talks were held between Afghan and Soviet delegations. Yakov Suritz, the Soviet representative, and Afghan Foreign Minister Mahmud Tarzi initialed the text of the Soviet-Afghan Friendship Treaty. An agreement was reached that Russia would provide Afghanistan with one million rubles in gold. In addition, twelve airplanes, with training of Afghan pilots and the establishment of an air school in Afghanistan, were granted, as well as aid in arming its national army. The Soviet government provided five thousand rifles with ammunition, built a smokeless powder factory, supplied equipment for a telegraph line to link Kushka, Herat, and Kandahar to Kabul, and sent technical and other specialists to Afghanistan.[7]

No matter how important this treaty was to Afghanistan, it was not signed quickly. But Russia did not cause the delay. Despite the civil war in the country, with attendant famine and devastation, Russia was ready to grant economic and military aid to Afghanistan. The ratification of the treaty was postponed several times by Afghan authorities because of strong opposition against better relations with the Soviets. Some of the emir's close associates wanted instead to improve relations with Britain. They claimed that without British support, Afghanistan could hardly hope to get worldwide recognition.

On March 9, 1920, British Indian Viceroy Chelmsford offered to resume English-Afghan negotiations. The talks went on between April 17 and July 24, 1920. The aim of the talks was not reached, because Britain was not in a hurry to recognize Afghan sovereignty. The issue of allowing an Afghan ambassador in London remained unresolved. A treaty was signed but only preliminarily.

The problem went back to World War I when Britain insisted on Afghan neutrality. In connection with this, Britain demanded that Afghanistan should refrain from any military and economic ties with Soviet Russia and expel Soviet diplomatic representatives from the country. If Afghanistan should accept the British terms, it would be granted twenty thousand rifles, twenty field batteries of artillery, arms for twenty machine-gun companies, as well as annual subsidies worth four million rupees and another forty million rupees over the next twenty-five years. In addition, Afghanistan would enjoy duty-free transit of its goods through British India. If all this was agreed to, Afghanistan would be able to have its representation in London.

The Soviet reaction to the British proposals was a note to the Afghan government that read in part: "We are aware of the efforts that British representatives are making to turn Afghanistan against Russia while the Afghan government adamantly refuses to embark on a road of hostility with the Russian Republic."[8]

British attempts to turn the Afghans to their side were fruitless, as the Soviets predicted. The British demand that the Soviet mission be banned from Kabul was rejected by the Afghan government. Letters by Amanullah Khan to Lenin of November 6 and December 1, 1920, are illustrative of the importance that Afghan leaders attributed to their relations with Soviet Russia. Most illustrative is the letter of December 1, 1920, in which Amanullah Khan said that he was sure that friendship between the Soviets and Afghans ". . . in the future would become even stronger and steadier."[9]

The development of increasing relations between the two countries required that a friendship treaty between them be signed as quickly as possible; such a treaty was signed in Moscow on February 28, 1921. Results were fast in coming. Only one week later, the request of the People's Commissariat on Foreign Affairs of the Russian Federation to provide Afghanistan with 120,000 rubles in gold was approved. On March 29, Lenin signed a resolution of the Council of People's Commissars by which 750,000 rubles were granted to the People's Commissariat of Finance of the Russian Federation for disbursement to Afghanistan.

For his part, Emir Amanullah Khan, understanding the importance of the Soviet-Afghan treaty, on August 7, 1921, called a jirga, a meeting of representatives of different regions of the country, as well as the khans of different tribes, landowners, rich merchants, and Moslem religious leaders. Discussion on the ratification of the treaty between those in favor of the improvement of Soviet-Afghan relations and those in opposition was very heated indeed. After four days of discussions on the Soviet-Afghan treaty and the draft of the proposed British-Afghan treaty, on August 11, 1921, the jirga finally ratified the Soviet-Afghan treaty by a majority vote. On August 13 the treaty was adopted formally by the government, and on August 14 by the emir.[10]

The significance of the treaty was not only that it formed a good basis for partnerlike and mutually advantageous relations between the two neighboring countries on a long-term basis, but also that Central Asian states were being introduced into the system of international relations as equal partners. The most important aspect was that the parties obligated themselves not to have military or political agreements with third powers if such agreements could cause harm to either of them.

History has most convincingly shown how wise both parties were in this concept. For instance, in the years of World War II, Nazi Germany fruitlessly tried to turn Afghanistan against the Allies. Even after the war, Afghanistan was staunchly neutral, not associating itself with any military faction.

Put directly in the treaty was that the young Soviet state declared itself ready to assist the Afghan people economically in all possible ways. According to the treaty of 1921, the Soviet government on March 12, 1921, made the first payment of 120,000 rubles in gold as economic help. The next payment in gold occurred in August. On November 7, twenty-six specialists arrived in Kabul from Soviet Russia. By the end of 1923 the Soviet government had fully fulfilled its other obligations under the treaty. For their part, Afghan authorities, learning of food shortages in some regions of Soviet Russia, in September 1921 declared their readiness to sell 500,000 poods (16 kilograms each) of wheat and 100,000 sheep to Russia. On November 27, 1921, the emir informed the Soviet representative that he was giving those starving in the region of the Volga River 200,000 poods of wheat free of charge.

New and larger opportunities for cooperation between the two countries in politics, economy, and culture were opening. Several days after signing the treaty, Ambassador Extraordinary of Afghanistan to Russia Gen. Muhammed Wali Khan, finally fulfilling the wish of Amanullah Khan, left Moscow for Western Europe with all possible assistance by the Soviet government. Soon, countries such as Germany, France, and Italy acknowledged Afghanistan's independence.

With the signing of the Soviet-Afghan treaty, the mission of Yakov Z. Suritz in Kabul was established and Fyodor Raskolnikov was appointed plenipotentiary representative of Soviet Russia. On April 15, 1921, he and his staff left Moscow for Afghanistan. Raskolnikov was a prominent bolshevik and official of the new Soviet state. He was trusted personally by Lenin. Undoubtedly, his appointment as the first Soviet ambassador to Afghanistan signified the great importance that the Soviet leadership attributed to developing good relations with Afghanistan. The varied interests and abilities of this man as a diplomat and his intellectual character greatly helped in making Russia and Afghanistan closer to each other. Raskolnikov was the first Soviet diplomat to be given an award by a foreign state. The Party's Central Committee allowed this diplomat-Communist to accept the award from the royal hand of Afghanistan's emir.

The official guidance for the new representative included summaries of major objectives and directions of Soviet foreign policy in the east, particularly those concerning Afghanistan. Raskolnikov was instructed that he should take into account the reformist program of the emir and not consider Afghanistan as an economically developed country. The instruction read:

> You by all means must avoid the deadly mistake of artificially imposing our ideas. We say to the Afghan government: we have one type of society and you have another; we have certain ideals and you have some others; but we are common in our striving for full independence and self-management of our two peoples. We do not interfere in your home affairs, we do not create obstacles for your people's life. We assist and support anything that plays a progressive role in the development of your people. Not for a single minute do we plan to impose on your people a program which is alien to them.[11]

It is impossible to ignore the international significance of the Soviet-Afghan treaty of 1921, particularly where it concerns Britain's changing position toward Afghanistan. On November 22, 1922, a final peace treaty between Great Britain and Afghanistan was signed. It provided that Britain acknowledge Afghanistan's independence and establish mutual diplomatic relations with embassies in London and Kabul.[12] This treaty differed greatly from the preliminary one, signed in Rawalpindi. The Afghan government, however, agreed to British demands not to open Soviet consulates in Kandahar and Ghazni, which were provisions of the Soviet-Afghan treaty of 1921. Instead, Afghanistan gained the right of transit of weapons and combat equipment through British India.[13]

The advent of this Anglo-Afghan treaty caused changes in relations between Afghanistan and other western states. The Soviet magazine *New East* (*Novi y Vostok*) wrote in 1922:

A new phase of the policies of European states in the east is beginning, a policy of half acknowledgment and half support. . . . Signing the treaty gave these countries a free hand. An Italian embassy was established in Kabul. France has a priority to send an ambassador there. Even Japan is beginning to show interest in Afghanistan. . . . France has surprised the world with its readiness to pay for Afghan students' studies in Paris, while Italy is training Afghan pilots.

It is noteworthy that this was a period of rivalry between European countries and Soviet Russia, competition for Afghanistan's friendship. Britain and some other European countries accused Russia of expansionism in its relations with Afghanistan, with a desire to occupy its territory and spread communist ideology there, while arming certain segments of the population with the goal of overthrowing the regime. In connection with this, the People's Commissar for Foreign Affairs, G. V. Chicherin, granted an interview to the French newspaper *L'Humanité*, published on July 24, 1921. In this interview he addressed European readers with the following words:

You do not understand enough of our policy in the East. They claim in the West that we are expansionists as far as territories in Asia are concerned. We are accused of being heirs of the tzarist economic policy. There is nothing that could be more wrong. We are strong and influential in Asia because we have given up any policy of aggrandizement. Peoples of the East view us as their friend because we are not imperialists any longer.

On September 15, 1921, the British government through its representative in Moscow sent a note to the Soviet government that accused the Soviets of anti-British propaganda in Turkey, Iran, Afghanistan, and India. In spring 1923, the official British representative in Russia handed a memorandum to Deputy People's Commissar for Foreign Affairs M. M. Litvinov that contained demands concerning alleged anti-British activities of Russia's representatives in Afghanistan. These included the demand that Soviet ambassadors should be called back from Iran and Afghanistan. The ultimatum was turned down.

For its part the Russian government accused Britain of attempts to destroy Afghanistan's sovereignty, arm insurgent tribes, instigate rebellion against the central government, and provoke terrorist attacks against Soviet representatives in Afghanistan.

In 1924, an antigovernment rebellion did occur in Afghanistan in which opposition-minded tribes fought against the emir. Russian newspapers exposed a plot of British secret services' participation in seeking to overthrow the uncooperative emir. The papers reported seizure by British authorities on the Indo-Afghan border of weapons and equipment bought by the emir's government from Italy and Germany. The rebellion was soon suppressed by troops loyal to the Afghan government.

The Afghan government was interested in the stability of relations with Soviet Russia. Afghanistan proposed a treaty of neutrality and nonaggression between the two countries. This was agreed to by the Soviets, with the signing taking place on August 31, 1926, in Paghman, near Kabul. The Paghman pact was of great significance for both countries. The traditional Afghan policy of neutrality was legitimized in an international treaty. Thus, the political independence of the country and its international authority were strengthened. The Paghman pact was the second in significance after the Soviet-Afghan treaty of friendship of 1921.

Meanwhile, the developing Soviet-Afghan relationship was having problems of its own. Heated debates occurred on both sides in the areas of policy, economy, and borders. For example, a difficult situation occurred in the two countries' relations because of a border incident and subsequent dispute about the island of Urta-Tugai in the Amu-Darya River. In late 1925, Soviet local troops caused Afghan posts to withdraw from the island. In fact, the territory for many years had been the island of Bukhara, and later was incorporated into the territory of the Tadzhik Soviet Republic. The western press wrote that the Soviet government ordered troops to occupy the island and join it to Soviet Asia by force.

After many meetings of representatives of the two countries, on August 1, 1926, a protocol on establishing a joint Soviet-Afghan commission on the matter was signed. On August 15 this commission agreed to its own protocol, which contained the provision that the Soviet Union was aware of the overwhelming importance of the economic interests of Afghanistan in the island of Urta-Tugai. This was based on unchanging friendship between the peoples of the two countries, with the aim of further improving the relationship. The Soviets agreed to a full transfer of the island to the jurisdiction of the Afghan government. For its part, Afghanistan was to take all necessary measures to prevent the island from being used by elements hostile to the Soviet Union or as a base for any assault on Soviet territory.[14]

This agreement was solid evidence of the two parties being able to solve such complicated problems peacefully, showing that in competition for Afghanistan, the winner was the Soviet Union and not Great Britain. The visit to the USSR of Afghan Emir Amanullah Khan in May 1928 was a further manifestation of this fact. The visit drew considerable attention worldwide, because this was the first time since the Soviets came to power that a head of a nation, and a monarchy at that, paid an official state visit to the new Communist country. This visit was an important part of the tour of the Afghan king to various Asian and European countries. Taking place between December 1927 and June 1928, the tour strengthened Afghan independence, widened contacts with European and Asian countries, and, perhaps of greatest importance, invited foreign capital to invest in the Afghan economy and thus ensure development of the country's international economic ties. "I am going to Europe for two reasons," Amanullah Khan announced on board the ship sailing from Egypt to Italy. "First, I want to make available to my country the best of everything that they have in Europe and, second, to show the countries of Europe that Afghanistan has its own place in the world."[15]

Amanullah Khan stayed in the Soviet Union for two weeks, May 2–18, 1928, where he met with Michael Kalinin, chairman of the All-Union Central Executive Committee, and Georgi Chicherin, People's Commissar for Foreign Affairs, as well as other important officials. He toured plants, child day-care centers, schools, and hospitals. While staying in Leningrad, Amanullah Khan met a delegation of Soviet Moslems headed by the chairman of the Central Religious Administration, Mufti Sahridinov.

In the course of meetings and talks with Soviet officials, extremely important questions of bilateral relations were considered. Amanullah Khan insisted on building a highway to connect the two countries. It was agreed that economic and cultural ties would be expanded, that

Soviet scientists would be sent to Afghanistan, and that various border disputes would be settled.[16]

Soon, both countries mutually agreed to join the Kellogg Pact, an international convention that prescribed the rejection of war as a means of national policy. By joining this pact, the USSR and Afghanistan demonstrated unity of principle, which the countries agreed to follow in foreign policy.

Economic factors have been important to both sides since the very beginning of Soviet-Afghan relations. The Socialist Revolution in Russia in 1917 caused a tradition to develop that had new forms and new quality. Although tzarist Russia also played a considerable role in Afghan foreign trade, decisive positions in Afghan markets were definitely with the British. The portion of trade through the Indo-Afghan border, for example, in 1911–1915 came to 62 percent of the country's overall volume of foreign trade. Along the Russian-Afghan border it was only 38 percent.[17]

Britain had no rivals in trade to the south of the Hindu Kush Mountains, whereas tzarist Russia was similarly situated to the north of it. Foreign trade became the only form of economic ties between Afghanistan and other countries, except for British donations to the emir.

Russian-Afghan trade during the civil war in Russia (1918–1921) almost stopped for lack of necessary goods in Central Asia. The situation was worse during World War I and especially in 1917, when Central Asia became isolated from Russia. In 1917–1923 Afghan trade across the Russian border came to only 2 to 3 percent of the overall volume of foreign trade. It reflected negatively on the state of the Afghan economy and the life of the population, especially in the northern regions of the country, where severe deprivation of necessities imported from Russia was felt. At the same time excess stores of cotton, wool, astrakhan,* and carpets grew, although some of them were exported to India. It was obvious that the quickest possible normalizing of Soviet-Afghan trade was of the greatest importance in relations between the two countries.

In solving this problem, the beginning of operation of the railroad between Kerki and Termez was of great help, along with Afghanistan

---

*Persian lamb; karakul.

being granted certain privileges by the Soviet government. Among these were the lifting of all limits for Afghan commerce to Soviet Russia, permitting the export from Russia of five hundred poods of sugar annually, and at the same time free and unlicensed import of all Afghan goods. The Soviet government canceled taxes for important Afghan export goods, such as astrakhan, lambskin, wool, leather, fruit, and carpets. Afghan merchants faced no obstacles on their goods entering Russia and were granted the right to open offices in some cities of the country.

The great fair in Nizhni Novgorod was also very important. Afghan merchants participated in it for the first time in 1925. This occurred by a special invitation sent by the Soviet government to Kabul on June 25, 1925, informing the Afghans that conditions for Afghan participation in the fair, to be conducted from August 1 through September 15, 1925, were unusually favorable: unlimited and unlicensed import to the USSR of Afghan goods and export from the USSR of any goods bought at the fair, fewer transport tariffs for railroad and sea and river transport, as well as freedom from certain special fees charged to other participants.[18] Because of these favorable conditions, the fair attracted a growing number of Afghan tradesmen with each passing year.

In the early 1920s the volume of Soviet-Afghan trade was still insignificant, actually less than that in the time of tzarist Russia. But, it was increasing every year and came to be an important factor of economic life in the northern regions of Afghanistan. The fact that Afghan merchants could sell Soviet goods without difficulty contributed to this.

From 1925 to 1926 the structure of Soviet exports to Afghanistan began to change. Some new items appeared in small quantities that were not part of prerevolutionary business, such as cement, electrical equipment, mechanical equipment for workshops, and farming machines. The need of the Soviet Union for such Afghan exports as cotton, wool, and leather became a stimulus for developing various branches of industry. Afghan agriculture exports overall also were attractive to Soviet importers.

In addition to trade, the Soviet state attached great significance to other forms of economic cooperation. For example, on August 14, 1920, a special detachment to set up a radio station arrived in Kabul, as economic assistance to the Afghan government. Courses for training Afghan pilots were established in Tashkent and, concurrently, the Soviet government presented Afghanistan with twelve planes.

From 1924 to 1925, under the instruction and participation of Soviet specialists, the telegraph line from Kushka to Herat to Kandahar to Kabul was constructed. This line, which still exists today, ensured reliable communications from Kabul to major cities in the entire country, as well as the Soviet Union and British India.

In 1927–1928, with the help of Soviet specialists, a cotton-processing plant and electric power station were built in Herat, using Soviet equipment in both cases. So, all during the 1920s, we see business contacts between the two countries increasing in industry, agriculture, science, and technology. In August 1923 Afghanistan was a participant in the first agricultural exhibition organized in Moscow. In May 1928, an Afghan delegation headed by the minister of commerce, Abdul Hadi Khan, visited the Soviet Union. The delegation toured a textile plant, an electric power station in Shatura, the Academy of Agriculture, and other plants, factories, and cultural institutions in Moscow. In June 1928 the first exhibition of Soviet-produced goods was held in Kabul.

On November 28, 1927, in Kabul, the USSR and Afghanistan signed an agreement setting up regularly scheduled air flights from Tashkent to Kabul.[19] In October 1928 the Soviet and Afghan governments agreed that the Soviets would provide help in building the Kabul to Termez highway. This important project was completed in 1929 and still is in use today.

Economic relations between Afghanistan and the Soviet Union were expanding, so the Afghan king had many items to discuss when he visited Moscow in May 1928. His talks with the Soviet government produced positive results, and new opportunities for expanded economic and cultural cooperation between the two countries were outlined.[20]

After his stay in Moscow, Amanullah Khan visited Turkey and Iran, where important agreements of friendship and cooperation between Afghanistan and those countries were signed.

As a whole, the trip of the Afghan king was very fruitful. It contributed to expanding foreign relations of Afghanistan, and provided opportunities for major changes in the economic and internal life of the country.

After returning home, Amanullah Khan started working out a new series of reforms, with the aim of eliminating all remnants of feudalism. In late August 1928, he announced his projects of new reforms at a Loya Jirga in Paghman. By these reforms, major feudal and tribal leaders would be deprived of various privileges. The new reforms weakened the positions of those religious figures who tended to undermine the reformist spirit of the government's policy. All mullahs had to have their qualifications renewed. The king and his cabinet tried also to start to modernize family relations, fixing the minimum age for marriage. In October at a high officials' (durbars') meeting, the king's government introduced new ideas of reform in social and everyday life, including joint schools for boys and girls, providing for Afghan youth to study abroad, and freeing women from purdah, the Moslem custom of women wearing veils.

Questions of economic development occupied an important place in the program of the Mlado-Afghan government. It tried to limit the influence of foreign capital, which monopolized both foreign and internal trade. The government formulated a policy of protecting the interests of local merchants. Commercial firms began to appear in the country, in whose activities representatives of the ruling circles invested, including the emir himself. These firms were granted the exclusive right to store and sell some of the most important goods.

The Mlado-Afghan reform program also included some important measures in the sphere of the military. Proposing that the Afghan army should be modernized in the European manner, Amanullah Khan insisted on instituting conscription instead of an all-volunteer force, increasing the initial length of service from two to three years, and forbidding the practice of one man serving for another for cash payments or any other reason. To finance the cost of the purchase of weapons abroad, Amanullah Khan in October 1928 decreed an extraordinary tax of five afghani for all citizens.[21]

Naturally, the reforms of Amanullah Khan became more and more unpopular with the people who were most affected by them. In the circle of the close advisors to the king, differences in views as to the scope and scale of reforms were increasing. There was a lack of political unity where the personal rivalry of the different leaders thrived. The progressive character of Amanullah Khan's reforms caused the number of his opponents to increase. The king's attempts to create a party called Istiklyal' va tadgaddot ("independence and renovation") as a political basis for modernization was blocked by the resistance

of a group of influential leaders of Young-Afghans who did not adhere to his radical views. Fearing this opposition in the highest echelons of power, Amanullah Khan deposed all those he considered
unreliable. Among them were major statesmen of the Young-Afghan
orientation. For example, among those who were forced to resign were
the minister of foreign affairs, Young-Afghan ideologist Mahmud Tarzi,
and one of the closest advisors of the king, Defense Minister Muhammed
Wali Khan, who headed the first Afghan diplomatic mission to Moscow in 1919. They were replaced by people with no clear political
orientation but who had managed to gain the king's trust. But even
some of his new advisors openly expressed their negative attitudes toward
the king's reforms. Around Amanullah Khan there was an atmosphere
of intrigue, mistrust, hostility, and fractionism.

The broad organized resistance of Young-Afghan elements arrayed
against the king became clear in the autumn of 1928. One major faction against Amanullah Khan consisted of certain Moslem leaders. He
was declared by them to be an atheist and a heretic, alleging that he
was abandoning the sacred principles of Islam, following instead those
infidels who did not believe in Allah. In a Moslem country such as
Afghanistan, this kind of opposition could be enough to shake the throne.
As the religious leaders became more of a major force in the
antigovernment movement, they were joined by other important conservative factions. The tribes' khans and other feudals disliked the limiting
of administrative power at a local level because this deprived them
of various privileges and reduced the volume of tax-free trade with
British India. This movement was supported also by the majority of
poor peasants who were gaining nothing from the social policies of
the government. On the contrary, by increasing the status of the bourgeois
class, their economic situation worsened. Tax on land skyrocketed,
reaching by the late 1920s 45 percent of the value of the harvest.[22]

Peasants, driven to despair by the khans cheating them, organized
themselves in detachments and robbed rich merchants and landowners. One of the strongest such bands was headed by a modern-day Robin
Hood, Habibullah, nicknamed Bacha-i Saqao ("son of a water carrier"),
who had deserted from the army. His people began to ambush representatives of local authorities and mercantile convoys, with part of what
was taken from them distributed among the poor.

In November 1928 some Pushtun tribes in the eastern province rebelled.

This insurrection spread rapidly, with army soldiers beginning to resist the authority of their officers.

At the end of 1928, two regions under insurrection were prominent, the southeastern and northern. In the east, the khans and mullahs of the Shinwari tribe on November 29 began to blockade Jalalabad and sent a special regiment to attack Kabul. Muhammed Omar Khan, grandson of former Afghan Emir Sher Ali Khan, joined the rebellion. While these events were taking place, Amanullah Khan became more convinced that the rebellion was being inspired by the British.[23]

By the end of December, the situation of the government forces worsened. On January 7, 1929, armed forces of Bacha-i Saqao smashed the emir's frontline troops and began to advance toward the capital. King Amanullah Khan, seeing no better course of action, abdicated the throne in favor of his elder brother, Inayatullah Khan. His earlier attempts to have talks with Bacha-i Saqao had been fruitless. On January 15, 1929, the rebels occupied Kabul; three days later Bacha-i Saqao was declared the emir of Afghanistan under the name Habibullah Khan Ghazi.

Thus ended one of the most important periods of progressive development in Afghanistan under the conditions of complete independence. During this time, Soviet-Afghan relations rose to a very high level of friendship and cooperation in many areas. This new revolution meant the return of the country to the old feudal routine. Soviet-Afghan relations became disrupted and grew worse with each passing day. Bacha-i Saqao's government affirmed its agreements between the USSR and Afghanistan, but in reality its actions contradicted them all. Saqao's government created favorable conditions for the activities of counterrevolutionary emigrants, and supplied them with weapons. The Soviet government was naturally disturbed at these developments and protested various infractions to the government of Bacha-i Saqao. In particular the Soviets addressed hostile activities of the *basmach* (Moslem guerrillas) military detachments and their violations of the border with Afghan authorities' knowledge and consent. Bacha-i Saqao refused these overtures, with his political actions leading to a diminution of Soviet-Afghan relations.

Having seized power, Emir Bacha-i Saqao did his best to annul the reforms of the former emir. The departments of justice, education, and schools were closed. Judicial procedures were relegated to religious courts. National industry slowed to a low level, and foreign and internal trade was paralyzed and prices escalated. Those who were adherents of Amanullah Khan and many merchants had their belongings confiscated.

Discontent with the new Bacha-i Saqao regime immediately followed in the country. The peasantry felt cheated by government promises, and other ordinary people became unhappy. A group of young Afghans began an armed struggle against the Bacha-i Saqao regime in Mazar-i-Sharif province.

By spring 1929 the British realized that Bacha-i Saqao was unable to provide for British interests in Afghanistan. This was demonstrated by the visit of the defense minister in the former emir's government, Muhammed Nadir Khan, to British India. With the help of the British colonial authority, Muhammed Nadir Khan managed to organize an armed unit of about 12,000 men and lead it against Kabul. Early in October 1929 the unit captured Kabul, and on October 15, Muhammed Nadir Khan was proclaimed emir at a meeting of his supporters. Bacha-i Saqao surrendered to the new authorities and was executed on November 1, 1929.

The Soviet Union did not interfere in the civil war of its neighboring country, although it more than once reiterated its adherence to the signed agreements. But after the Afghan civil war, relations between the Soviet Union and Afghanistan began to improve. More active trade was the best testimony to it. The Soviet Union, taking into consideration the fact that Afghanistan badly needed foreign currency, imported goods with payments in gold instead of having to resort to barter deals. The Soviet Union allowed Afghan national merchants their own representatives in Soviet territory and permitted them to open offices both in Moscow and in Middle Asia.

As the world economic crisis due to the great depression deepened, Soviet-Afghan trade exchanges continued to grow. The Soviet share in Afghan foreign trade increased and in 1938 and 1939 it improved by 24 percent. Soviet imports from Afghanistan were mainly wool, furs (lambskin and sheepskin), astrakhan, cattle, cotton, oil-bearing seeds, carpets, raisins, and almonds.

The Nadir Khan government was able to sign a trade agreement with the USSR and in doing so it referred to the economic weakness of Afghan merchants. The statement said that it feared competition once foreign traders gained access to the Afghan market.[24]

USSR-Afghan economic relations were not limited to trade. For example, the Soviet Union helped Afghanistan in creating its cotton-processing industry. Four large and seven smaller factories were built in Imam-Sahib, Taliqan, Hodgi-Har, Daulatabad, Baghlan, and Mazar-i-Sharif. In 1938 the largest cotton-processing factory was built in Kunduz. It processed more than 10,000 tons of cotton a year, and there were special shops at the factory producing oil and soap.

But, unfortunately, Soviet-Afghan relations in those days failed to achieve a stable character. There were certain outstanding problems that caused distrust and criticism. One example was Afghan participation with Turkey, Iran, and Iraq in the so-called Saadab Pact, concluded on July 8, 1937, in Teheran. This treaty stipulated the need to try to restrain the expansionist policy of the Soviet Union.

There was no stability in the internal life of Afghanistan, either. An active opposition surfaced that resented the cruel prosecution of Amanullah Khan's former supporters. Nadir Khan was assassinated in November 1933 by one of Amanullah Khan's supporters. Nadir Khan's son, Muhammad Zahir Shah, succeeded his father to the throne.

The new emir did not introduce any changes in the cabinet, nor were any policies changed. The process of centralizing and concentrating the national capital accelerated. During the late 1930s the role of the Afghan National Bank increased. It regulated foreign trade operations, thus exerting pressure on overall monetary policy. Abdul Majid, president of the bank, was appointed economic minister in 1938. These actions stimulated foreign ties, including those with the Soviet Union.

In the late 1930s the international situation became tense. Taking into consideration the territorial proximity of Afghanistan to the Soviet Union, Fascist Germany and other Axis countries made every effort to intensify their influence there. German-Afghan contacts were widened. In 1937 Afghanistan was provided a loan worth 27 million marks to buy German products, and as a result German military equipment was sent to Afghanistan. Hitler's agents, working as "advisors" or "consultants," infiltrated Afghan state institutes and industrial enterprises, including the national bank.

The Zahir Shah regime, while increasing ties with Germany and its allies, did not accede to any military-political obligations with the Nazis. Shortly after World War II began in September 1939, Afghanistan formally declared its neutrality. Despite this attitude, Germany continued trying to turn Afghanistan into a bridgehead for military activities against the USSR and British India. Its agents approached the Pushtun tribes' region in the south as well as the northwestern strip of India, supplying weapons and money. In 1940, Germany tried to talk the Afghan government into provoking a riot in the northwestern part of India against British rule, with the goal of forcing Britain to withdraw part of its troops from Europe. In return, Afghanistan would be given a chance to expand its territory at the expense of India, particularly in Sind, Baluchistan, western Punjab, and Kashmir. The Afghan government rejected this idea.

But Afghanistan's policy of maneuvering between Germany and other western countries created favorable conditions for activities of German intelligence. Nazi agents working under the disguise of merchants and consultants expanded anti-Soviet activity, organizing terrorist bands from former White-Guard emigrants who were residing in Afghanistan. These insurgents were sent into Soviet territory to create confusion.

This continuous activity of German intelligence agents in Afghan territory jeopardized its neutrality and ran counter to the Soviet-Afghan 1931 treaty on neutrality and nonaggression. In October 1941, the Soviet government called on the Afghan government to immediately stop the anti-Soviet activity of the various German agents. The British government made a similar appeal.

As a result of these appeals, Afghan authorities decided to expel from the country German and Italian subjects who were not part of the accredited diplomatic corps. They soon left Afghanistan.

A congress of the Loya Jirga was held in Kabul in November 1941 to work out a viable foreign policy under the complicated circumstances of World War II. The policy of Afghan neutrality was unanimously reiterated, but diplomatic links with Germany and Italy were retained intact during the war. After the war was over, on May 30, 1945, the governments of the United States, Great Britain, France, and the USSR demanded that the members of the German mission in Kabul be interned. The Afghan government met the Allies' demand and in August 1945 personnel of the German mission were turned over to Soviet authorities. Before this, Soviet-Afghan contacts between 1940 and 1945 had regressed to information exchanges only.

The defeat of Fascist Germany by the Soviet Union and its allies, the United States and Great Britain, removed the threat of an occupation by Hitler's army of eastern countries, including Afghanistan. German General Staff documents as well as memories of its generals published in the postwar period leave no doubt that Hitler had planned to turn Iran, Afghanistan, Turkey, India, and other countries into German colonies. The General Staff chief, Col. Gen. Franz Halder, wrote in his war diary on November 25, 1939, that Hitler had ordered plans to prepare for future war theaters in Asia, including Afghanistan.

The Supreme Command headquarters' directive No. 32 is a testimony to Hitler's aggressive plans concerning the Oriental countries. The directive's caption read, "In preparation for the period after the Barbarossa plan has been carried out, the Wehrmacht top-priority strategic plans under this directive are an occupation of middle east and southwest Asian countries. (Top secret! For commanding personnel only!)"[25] Aggression against southwest Asian countries was to be launched from the Soviet Caucasus across Iran and Afghanistan into India. In January 1945, when the outcome of the war was clear, the Soviet government addressed a message to the government of Afghanistan that thanked them for adherence to the 1931 treaty and its provisions during the war. The Soviet Union expressed its willingness to develop traditional relations between the two countries. The Afghan government welcomed these propositions.

The war's interference with traditional economic and trade links dealt a severe blow to the Afghan economy. Large amounts of agricultural products, such as cotton, wool, and fruit, had accumulated in warehouses. The sagging national industry was unable to cope with it. Manufactured goods were in great demand, but the import of industrial equipment had stopped completely. Inflation was rampant, with the prices of food and industrial goods soaring. Wide sections of the population—peasants, artisans, and the petty bourgeoisie—were the worst hit. Export of capital for safekeeping by the royal family and powerful landlords had occurred. To some extent, this corruption was caused by the instability of the dynasty's regime. Under the circumstances, as the internal situation in the country deteriorated, the potential for democratic reforms was gaining strength.

The struggle for democratic reforms embraced all spheres of life, state management, economy, and culture. The movement known as the Awakened Youth ("Wikh-e-Zalmayan") was most active, uniting progressive representatives of petty and middle bourgeoisie. In the early 1950s several political groups in opposition to the government began to publish the first private newspapers. These groups either came from the Awakened Youth movement or formed around it. The number of supporters for democratic reforms was constantly growing as new democratic forces became involved in the struggle. A landowner from Kandahar, Muhammed Rassul Khan, a Pushtun, headed the movement. Nur Muhammed Taraki, who led the radical left wing, Abdurauf Benawa, Abdulhai Habibi, and Gul Pacha Ulfat were prominent activists. At first they were engaged in educational propaganda, but by the late 1940s they joined the active political struggle, running in the parliamentary elections. As a result, a group of deputies, whose politics were based on Wikh-e-Zalmayan ideas, entered into the People's Council of the seventh convocation.

The movement's manifesto was based largely on political demands aimed at democratization of the state political system in combination with the alleviation of the people's low standard of living.

Another group that emerged in 1950 was known as Watan (home-land) and had similar attitudes but a wider spectrum of social-political and economic programs. The movement campaigned force-fully for democratization of political institutions through a revision of the constitution, adoption of a new law on the press, free parlia-mentary elections, the right to set up political parties and trade unions, revision of legal procedure, and separation of the three forms of power: legislative, executive, and judicial.

One faction's newspaper was called *Nida-i Khalq* ("The Voice of the People"). Judging by the social position of its members, it was closer to the democratic sector (intelligentsia, petty clerks, and arti-sans). Doctor Abdurahman Mahmudi was its founder, ideologist, and leader. Denouncing armed struggle, the *Nida-i Khalq* supporters based their political program on the ideas of democratic and social justice through electing a free parliament in a democratic election.

One form of the opposition struggle of the bourgeois democrats involved their parliamentary activities. While belonging to different political groups, their approaches to the key issues were either similar or very close. They unanimously accused the government of violating the constitution.

The activity of the opposition deputies failed to lead to any mean-ingful changes, however, either in the state management system or in the economic structure. But the pronouncements of the opposition groups in parliament and their published demands to a great extent determined the future political struggle within the public at large. In the summer of 1951 the *Nida-i Khalq* leaders made an effort to organize their supporters in a political party despite the fact that there was no law that allowed this.

Within *Nida-i Khalq,* party founder Doctor Mahmudi headed a cadre of ten people. But his party was not large and lacked the support of the people. The party's activity was concentrated mainly among the medicine and law students of Kabul University. It did not last long, only until the spring of 1952. Students, however, increased their involvement in the political struggle in the late 1940s and early 1950s.

The demands favored by middle-class people urged some representatives of the emir's circle to oppose the government. They united into a "National Club," whose founder and president was Sardar Muhammed Daud, the king's cousin. The club's activity was financed by a prominent Afghan merchant, the Afghan minister of economy, Abdul Majid Zabuli. Efforts to weaken the Muhmud-khan government sufficed for the group because they wanted to have Sardar Daud become the premier, replacing the incumbent Shah Mahmud.

The election of the eighth National Assembly in April 1952 was the peak of the activities of the various opposition groups. None of the opposition candidates was elected as a deputy. This fact prompted the leaders of the middle-class groups to arrange a mass demonstration in Kabul protesting the alleged rigging of the parliamentary election and the authorities' interference in the election campaign. Students in the capital led by Babrak Karmal* joined the demonstration, which was crushed by the military. The demonstration was followed by a wide-scale government purge against the opposition. Private newspapers were banned and opposition groups were smashed, with their leaders arrested and jailed. One of the opposition leaders, Nur Muhammed Taraki, was appointed press attaché of the Afghan Embassy in the USA. Later he became one of the ideologists of the Afghan People's Democratic Party and a leader of the 1978 April revolution. Despite the short length

*Babrak Karmal was one of the leaders of the 1978 April revolution in Afghanistan. He came to power as a result of deposing President Amin who was killed in 1979.

of time that the opposition was active, it produced a great impact on the country's social development.

There are no facts to show either ties or contacts between the Soviet Union and the Afghan opposition at that time. Soviet official circles may have feared that such contacts to some extent would jeopardize their valuable current and future foreign policy programs with the neighboring country. Bilateral relations in the first postwar years improved greatly. Border problems that had been disputed for years, and for which the Afghan side was very concerned, were getting settled. Under the June 13, 1946, treaty, the state border along the Amu-Darya and the Punja rivers was altered. The Soviet Union agreed to the Afghan request to move the border from the left bank of the Amu-Darya and the Punja to a line connecting the deepest points of the riverbed. This let Afghanistan begin navigating the river freely, thus allowing the population of the northern parts to use the waters of the rivers for irrigation, shipping, and fishing. A number of islands were transferred to Afghan sovereignty, and the Soviet Union lifted its ban on the use of Kushka River water and abandoned its right to build a dam on the Murghab using the Afghan bank.[26]

Due to poor economic performance and political instability in the country, there was a change of cabinet in 1953. Muhammed Daud, Emir Zahir Shah's cousin, took the post of prime minister. To strengthen the dynasty and its supporters, the new government reviewed some aspects of home policy that had been in force before 1953. It modernized and abandoned some obsolete state institutes and traditions. In the economy, Muhammed Daud proclaimed the so-called "guided economy," which instituted more highly controlled curbs on the financial-economic development of the country. Foreign policy was aimed at creating favorable conditions to strengthen the ruling dynasty's standing and build an image as the protector of the country's national interests. The principles of neutrality remained the basis of foreign policy.

Soviet-Afghan relations in the 1950s and 1960s were improving rapidly and could be described as friendly. The Soviet Union gave Afghanistan large credits to build a bread-producing factory in Kabul and provide amenities for the capital. The exchange of specialists and government delegations was made on a regular basis. A summit meeting was held in December 1955, when a Soviet delegation led by Chairman Nikita Khrushchev visited Afghanistan. A wide range of political, economic, and cultural issues was discussed. The Soviet government agreed to extend a long-term loan worth 100 million dollars for the economic development of Afghanistan.

A Soviet-Afghan agreement on technical assistance on construct-ing sixteen enterprises envisaged by the five-year plan was concluded in January 1956.[27] These included the Naghlu and Pul-i-Khumri hydroelectrostations, a car-repair plant, a nitro-fertilizer factory, three dams, the Jalalabad irrigation canal, airfields in Kabul and Bagram, highway across the Hindu Kush mountain range, and the Qizil Qala river port.[28]

The USSR hoped to help develop a technical-economic basis for the country's future. As a distinguishing feature of Soviet-Afghan economic cooperation, the Soviet Union at this time did not try to infringe on the sovereignty of the country's political situation. See Table I.[29]

Soviet-Afghan Trade in the 1950s

Year	Turnover (in millions of rubles)	Imports to Afghanistan	Exports from Afghanistan	Surplus
1951	41.9	20.0	21.9	+1.9
1954	72.7	32.9	39.8	+6.9
1955	98.1	43.7	54.4	+10.7
1956	133.5	60.5	73.0	+12.5
1957	155.2	82.7	72.5	-10.2
1958	142.7	50.4	92.5	+42.1
1959	175.8	62.4	113.4	+51.0

The Afghan National Economy Ministry favored import of manu-factured goods from the Soviet Union; thus the USSR became its biggest trade partner. Afghanistan received more than 50 percent of its im-ported machinery and equipment, 85 percent of its petroleum prod-ucts, and nearly 100 percent of its sugar and matches from the USSR. Afghanistan exported more than 60 percent of its cotton, 70 percent of its wool, 25 percent of its dried fruits and nuts, 40 percent of its oil-bearing seeds, and 40 percent of its goat- and sheepskins to the Soviet Union. Scientific and cultural ties were also growing.[30]

Soviet-Afghan relations in the 1960s can be described as stable. A gradual shift from the policy of confrontation and cold war to détente and cooperation was a major historic event in the world politics of that era. Afghanistan and other non-Allied countries played an important role in the process.

Dramatic changes in the international arena had their impact on Afghan home policy. Democratic tendencies were continuing to strengthen. A new constitution was adopted on October 1, 1964, in which the monarchy proclaimed further freedom and rights for Afghan subjects. Under the new constitution, for the first time women took part in the parliamentary election of 1965, with voting being secret. The right to establish and organize political parties was also proclaimed.

Certain opposition newspapers took an active part in helping to create a progressive public outlook, with the democratic intelligentsia united around them. The First (Constitutive) Congress of the Afghan People's Democratic Party (PDPA), a left-leaning socialist organization, was held illegally in Kabul on January 1, 1965. It consisted of a party of radical reform supporters from the intelligentsia, workers, and artisans. The congress elected the Central Committee, including seven members and four candidates. Nur Muhammed Taraki was elected general secretary of the party. Babrak Karmal, Keshtmand, and others became the Central Committee's members. The newspaper *Khalq* ("the people"), the organ of the PDPA, published the party's program in April 1966; it promulgated demands for deep democratic changes leading to social progress, and a democratic government that would meet the interests of the people. The program provided for the party's determination to fight for a state of national democracy and the country's transfer to a noncapitalist way of development, which eventually would create a basis for a socialist society. Revealing the class structure of the party, the newspaper wrote,

> . . . this new-type political organization would embrace the vanguard of the working class together with the peasantry and progressive intelligentsia, becoming a leading force of the democratic movement. The party aimed to unite the people in their struggle against despotism and reaction, to show the working people the way to a free and democratic society. . . .[31]

In the late 1960s, a different trend emerged in Afghanistan when its ideologists advocated the ideas of petty bourgeois extremism. Unlike the PDPA, they came out for a forcible seizure of power. Their slogan was "The gun brings power," with revolutionary peasants the force they counted on. The representatives of this group put forth their ideas in the newspaper *Shola-e Jaweid* ("eternal flame"). Doctor Hadi Mahmudi and engineer Muhammed Osman headed the faction. Their supporters were actively trying to win students to include high-school pupils as well as ethnic minorities, particularly in Herat and the Hazarajat. In May 1968 a story in *Shola-e Jaweid* helped to provoke a clash between the participants of a rally and the police. As a result, the leaders were arrested and the newspaper was banned.

The publication of a private newspaper, *Afghan Mellat* ("Afghan nation"), was a remarkable event in the country's political life in the second half of the 1960s. It helped unite the supporters of middle-class nationalist ideas who proclaimed themselves social democrats. Their leader and ideologist was the publisher of this newspaper, the energy department minister, and a future mayor of Kabul, Ghulam Muhammed Farhad. Farhad's years of study in Fascist Germany must have influenced his political outlook, because his ideas had much in common with those of national socialism. "A single national spirit" was viewed as a panacea for all social troubles.[32]

Another private newspaper, *Wahdat* ("unity"), voiced its concern over the people's social and economic troubles. It appealed for the unity of all classes in striving for social justice. The publishers of *Wahdat* rejected any forms of struggle.

The process of political liberalization tended to weaken the powers of the Moslem theologians. Stern ministers of religion, who had always backed the obsolete social economic order, began to lose their influence in various spheres of political life. But certain mullahs who came from middle-sized towns and had received more modern religious education, either at home or abroad, tried to develop the concept of a new Islam, its dogma adjustable to the demands of modern life. Their political views were formulated under the influence of different middle-class values, as well as socialist ideas that spread rapidly in Afghanistan, especially after the PDPA had been set up.

As Islam modernists learned some of these ideas, they found some of the early Islam tenets in tune with socialist doctrine, such as the ideas of equality and justice. They tried to show the compatibility of Moslem teaching with socialism, calling their conception "Islamic socialism."

Afghan traditional theologians, representing the main sects and orders, and the imams of the biggest mosques who were economically connected with the feudal landowners and large-scale traders, continued to oppose any changes capable of undermining traditional values and structures.

Thus, the overall ideological struggle for the manner of how the country should be developed involved all sectors of the population. Active political life, taking various forms, reflected mounting tensions in social relations. The people's standard of living remained low despite some advances in economic growth over the two five-year periods. Wealth tended to concentrate in the merchant class and did not trickle down to the lower classes.

In 1971, the economic crisis grew, with soaring prices, production slowdowns, bankruptcy of a large number of small entrepreneurs and artisans, and increases in the unemployment rate. This caused the political struggle to intensify to the point where Prime Minister Etemadi was forced to resign. In its place, the Dr. Abdul Zahir cabinet was set up.

Democratic forces, having very few seats in the parliament, did not have the power to initiate any legislation there. This caused the democrats to combine their political activities with those outside the parliament, such as the Afghanistan People's Democratic Party (PDPA) members who became most active with them. The extremist forces of the right, led by a group called The Moslem Brotherhood were becoming more and more strident. In May 1970, this group organized rallies and demonstrations in Kabul under slogans calling for jihad (holy war) against all democrats and socialists.

In 1971–1972 a new wave of strikes led by the PDPA swept Afghanistan. Workers of large factories went on strike, with peasants and artisans joining in. During these years, extremely bad droughts plunged the country into an economic recession that triggered political instability. Poor crops and loss of cattle followed the droughts, causing food shortages that were most painful. The tonnages of products coming from abroad, including the Soviet Union, were not big enough to solve the problem of a general lack of food. So, famine struck some of the most remote parts of the country. In the cities, rapid price increases on food were accompanied by speculation by major traders.

Mounting social unrest in combination with economic troubles required urgent and radical social and economic reforms. In a country without a massively supported political party capable of leading the opposition, the army itself plotted to do away with the doomed regime. On the night of July 16–17, 1973, a group of officers headed by former premier Muhammed Daud organized a bloodless coup d'état. The monarchy was abolished and Afghanistan was proclaimed a republic. The new regime was hailed by the military and the population of the city as further proof of the deposed monarchy's excessive unpopularity. King Muhammed Zahir Shah, who was in Italy at the time of the coup, abdicated. The Republican Central Committee became the supreme power body of the state. Most officers who had taken part in the coup became members of the committee.

Several political organizations were behind the antimonarchy coup. The PDPA, which formed the left wing of the republican regime, was among them. At the same time, the position of the antimonarchy opposition representing the ruling class was rather strong. It claimed that reforms were essential to accelerate the national bourgeois evolution if its power was to be strengthened. The group was headed by Muhammed Daud and his brother, Muhammed Naim. Although politically united at the first stage of the struggle, it was still a heterogeneous group of people that formed the ruling republican groups.

The Soviet Union naturally welcomed the new Afghan republic after the coup d'état. The Soviet leadership believed that if the country could acquire a socialist orientation, it would suit the objective of the USSR to keep Soviet-Afghan relations at a high level. Socialist political developments were of major importance in the wide-ranging ties between the two countries. Contacts at all levels intensified, thus stimulating Soviet-Afghan cooperation in various walks of life. The protocol extending the Soviet-Afghan 1931 treaty on neutrality and nonaggression for another ten years was signed in December 1975. The principles of equality, mutual respect for each other's sovereignty, independence, and noninterference in internal affairs were the foundation articles of the treaty. Cooperation in the international arena was an important part of the bilateral relations. Despite different economic systems, the two countries demonstrated their willingness to act jointly to bring about peace and security for the people of both countries.

Soviet-Afghan economic relations were definitely on the rise. By the end of 1977, with the help of Soviet economic and technical assistance, 115 industrial enterprises had been built or were in some advanced state of construction, with about 70 that had already been put into operation and were producing profits. The construction of oil storage facilities, roads, a large bakery, the international airport, the river port on the bank of the Punja River, and many other projects had come from Soviet investments.

It is remarkable that Soviet-Afghan relations happened to be upgraded after Afghanistan was proclaimed a republic. An agreement on trade and payments was signed on March 20, 1974, with most-favored-nation status for the Afghans reflected in the document. The Soviet Union and Afghanistan agreed to promote bilateral trade on the favorable terms they had already extended or would extend in the future to any third country.

For the first time in Soviet-Afghan trade relations, a specific long-term agreement on trade was signed on June 19, 1976. The accord spelled out the products to be exchanged over a five-year period and stipulated a 65 percent growth of trade between the two countries.

A continual flow of automobiles, cotton-processing equipment, tractors, bulldozers, concrete, glass, and other material was coming from the Soviet Union. Wool, leather, dried fruits, nuts, cotton, pomegranate juice, grapes, and figs were sent to the northern neighboring country. Afghan natural gas was another raw material used to reimburse the Soviet Union for its economic and technical assistance to Afghanistan.

In addition to the nonaggression pact and the two agreements on bilateral trade, a new major agreement on economic and technical cooperation was signed on February 27, 1977. The treaty was to last for a period of twelve years, but it was expected to be extended automatically for another five years, unless cancelled by either the USSR or Afghanistan.

Many Afghans were trained in technical skills, or received higher education in the Soviet Union. During the years from 1971 to 1974, 500 Afghan students were provided higher education in the USSR, about 22 percent of all the Afghan specialists who were educated abroad. The number of doctors trained in the Soviet Union was particularly high.

From the very early days of its rule, the Daud republican government announced its determination to carry out a series of reforms in the country. The nationalization of banks and the introduction of fixed working hours, paid leaves, improvements in the education system, and extended medical care all looked very promising. Despite the best of intentions, however, these reforms failed to bring about radical changes.

An especially significant reform that was of utmost importance for the common people of Afghanistan was land redistribution. The majority of the country's population lived in rural areas with only 40,000 landlords owning 60 percent of the arable land. At the same time 1.5 million peasants possessed only very small farms or no land at all. Unfortunately, the June 1973 military coup did not do much to improve the living conditions of the people or the social makeup of the nation. Discontent with the government's policies started to increase.

Since the mid-1970s, ripening internal social tensions began to exert pressure on the country's foreign policy. While maintaining its economic ties with the Soviet Union, the Daud government improved its relations with the ruling circles of some Middle East countries and Iran. Certain important economic programs were linked to financial aid from oil-producing countries. These developments hardly pleased the USSR. The Soviet government became greatly concerned over these new ties with other countries, fearing that Soviet-Afghan cooperation might lessen.

The Soviet Union condemned a campaign of repressions that Daud launched against the forces of the left. In a relatively short time after becoming president, he concentrated most of the power of the country in his own hands. A one-party system was proclaimed in Afghanistan, with the National Revolutionary Party (NRP)* holding the most important political prerogatives. The ascendancy of the NRP as a one-party system was much like the Communist Party of the USSR causing all other parties and groups to be banned. As a result, the PDPA had to go underground. This development was a real threat not only to the PDPA's activities but to its fundamental existence. Its two groups, Khalq and Parcham, worked together more closely to clear the way for the eventual unity of the party.

The surreptitious PDPA conference held in July 1977 set as its primary agenda the goal of deposing the Daud regime. Party members, abiding by the conference resolution, intensified their clandestine activity, especially in the army. Numerous mass organizations of workers, peasants, women, and youth were created in areas where the PDPA influence was very strong.

---

*NRP is the common Russian abbreviation for the socialist party approved enthusiastically by the USSR. In America and other western countries, it is commonly called the People's Democratic Party of Afghanistan (PDPA). Throughout this book, the Russian version will be used.

On the seventh of Saur 1357, according to the Afghan sun calendar, which corresponds to April 27, 1978, the Afghan military organized still another coup, in this case one from the left. President Daud, who refused to surrender to the revolutionary authorities, was killed in the takeover, and his cabinet and leaders of the NRP were arrested.

A Military Revolutionary Council (MRC) held power in the first days after the April (Saur) revolution. In its first proclamations, it addressed the Afghan people, proclaiming the final end of any vestiges of the monarchy and the start of a truly democratic national revolution. On April 29, the MRC passed its power to a Revolutionary Council and merged itself with the new governing body.

The Revolutionary Council proclaimed the formation of the Democratic Republic of Afghanistan (DRA) and elected Nur Muhammed Taraki as chairman of the Revolutionary Council and prime minister of the country. Babrak Karmal became his first deputy.

The first decrees of the new authorities showed their determination to lead the country along the way of socialist society, stressing social justice. Significant steps were undertaken to improve the well-being of working people, including a seven-hour working day for workers and clerks. To address long-standing grievances, land reform was initiated, which provided land to 300,000 peasant families. To control inflationary tendencies, measures were taken to bring down consumer prices, supply the people with necessities, and provide jobs for high-school graduates. A campaign to fight illiteracy was started.

But the people's enthusiasm for the new regime did not last very long. Socialist slogans proved to be incomprehensible for most citizens. Probably contributing most to their discontent was the fact that the new government sought to undermine the strong religious beliefs of the people, thus opposing their traditional way of life. This policy undermined the authorities' credibility. Many peasants refused to own the land they were provided because the Koran characterizes the appropriation of someone else's land as a sin.

A further struggle for power within the republic's leadership, coupled with a lack of unity, caused the situation to deteriorate. The mere taking of power did not and in fact could not improve the situation. Continuous discord, executions, and arrests were similar to those generated by Stalin in the Soviet Union in the 1930s. History was repeating itself.

Haste, inflexibility, and lack of continuity torpedoed the reform process. Individual projects blew up like soap bubbles, since they addressed neither concrete circumstances that needed solutions, nor reality. The Soviet leadership believed the difficulties to be only temporary. But it was naive to hope that the situation in Afghanistan would soon improve, because history frequently has shown that a revolutionary appeal is not enough to provide success on its own. A broad disinformation campaign was undertaken in Afghanistan in the late 1970s, with many politically inexperienced people from remote parts of the country falling victim to it. People were brainwashed with promises of a better life, a future with material abundance, a kind of paradise. In fact, very little had been accomplished to bring into being the goals of the April revolution. For this reason, it was doomed to failure.

The Soviet Union watched as the situation in Afghanistan continued to deteriorate, with results that could be unpredictable. In fact, the USSR could no longer control the situation in the neighboring country as it desired. Moreover, other countries, including the USA, had interests in the region also. From the Soviet viewpoint, something had to be done. How the situation in Afghanistan could be handled to their advantage was of great concern to many in the Kremlin.

One thing was certain to the Soviets. Afghanistan was not to be allowed to abandon its socialist orientation. Everything possible was to be done to maintain the situation and policies in the direction the Soviet Union desired. Soviet-Afghan ties had been generally friendly for many years, whether Afghanistan was a monarchy or a republic. Although there were periods of stagnation or even alienation, Soviet-Afghan relations had never been affected by any military conflicts or the use of force to settle disputes.

Despite this long history, in December 1979 Afghanistan fell victim to Soviet aggression, although the Soviet leaders tried to convince the world that there was no violation of international law. They endlessly reiterated that the Soviet Union had to take only a temporary step that had the sole aim of supporting the legitimate Afghan government, thus rebuffing counterrevolutionary forces.

Time will pass and things will be called by their proper names. The story is yet ahead.

NOTES

1. L. W. Adamec, *Afghanistan 1900–1923: A Diplomatic History* (Berkeley, CA: University of California Press, 1967), 110.
2. N. A. Halfin, "Questions of History," No. 6 (1980): 120.
3. A. Swinson, *North-Western Border, People and Events, 1839–1947* (London: 1967).
4. USSR Foreign Policy Documents: 1917–1980, Edition 4, Volume 1–6, Moscow, 1981, 175.
5. USSR Foreign Policy Documents, 204.
6. USSR Foreign Policy Documents, 204.
7. USSR Foreign Policy Documents, Vol. 3, 318.
8. USSR Foreign Policy Papers, Vol. 4, 94–95.
9. USSR Foreign Policy Papers, Vol. 4, 94–95.
10. USSR Foreign Policy Papers, Vol. 4, 94–95.
11. USSR Foreign Policy Papers, Vol. 4, 166–167.
12. See L. W. Adamec, *Afghanistan 1900–1923*, 157–166.
13. British and Foreign State Papers, Vol. 114, London, 1,944.
14. USSR Foreign Policy Papers, Vol. 10, 388.
15. Documents on National-Colonial Problems, Moscow, 1934, 85.
16. USSR Foreign Policy Papers, Vol. 2, 293.
17. Naum M. Gurevich, Afghan Foreign Trade Before the Second World War (Moscow: 1967).
18. USSR Foreign Policy Papers, Vol. 8, 390–391.
19. USSR Foreign Policy Papers, Vol. 10, 71.
20. USSR Foreign Policy Papers, Vol. 12, 144–145.
21. V. Gershkevich, *The Avestian Hymn to Mithra* (London: 1959).
22. P. Alekseenkov, *Agrarian Question in Afghan Turkestan* (Moscow: 1933), 32–33.
23. USSR Foreign Policy Papers, Vol. 11, 611.
24. *A Collection of the USSR Acting Treaties, Agreements, and Conventions with Foreign States,* 10th ed., 105–109.
25. Documents and data, Moscow, 1967, 199–203.
26. *A Collection of the USSR Acting Treaties, Agreements, and Conventions with Foreign States,* 13th ed. (Moscow: 1956), 262–266.

27. *Pravda*, March 5, 1956.
28. The Asian countries economic development projects. USSR Foreign Policy Documents, Vol. 10, 242–243.
29. *Modern Afghanistan* (Moscow: 1960), 406–407.
30. "Foreign Trade of the USSR," 1959, No. 8, 27.
31. *Khalq*, April 11, 1966. The authors are unsure of the role of the Soviet Communist party in the formation of the PDPA, but we assume that some support was given them, as in the cause of other such parties in other countries.
32. *Afghan Mellat,* April 26, 1969.

Chapter 2

HOLY WAR AGAINST THE UNFAITHFUL

————————

——

Today we can speak with great certainty and bitterness about the responsibility of the then leadership of the Soviet Union for the military invasion of Afghanistan and its consequences. Now, it is absolutely clear that the orders that put the military intervention in operation were issued without taking into account moral norms and international law. The decision seems to have been made in the Kremlin without consultation because of the underestimation of the power of the *Mujahidin* (holy warriors) to the socialist regime and the strength of the opposition. The rebel Afghan groups, called loosely Mujahidin, were referred to with disdain as bandit groupings, terrorists, and *dushmans* ("enemies"). The Soviet leadership was sure that if only the Soviet troops would step into the territory of Afghanistan, coming "at the call of brothers in the class struggle," the opposition would immediately become manageable. The People's Democratic Party of Afghanistan (PDPA) supported by its army would then have the situation under its control. It would have achieved unity in its ranks and would have been on the road toward successfully fulfilling its socioeconomic program. The Soviet leadership assumed, erroneously, that use of Soviet military force in Afghanistan would allow it to quickly suppress all resistance and in the meantime strengthen the Afghan army, which would then have been able to act by itself and permit the Soviet troops to return home.

This was one of the major miscalculations of the Soviet leadership. The Soviet troops' invasion of Afghanistan actually stirred up the whole country. Different groups making up the opposition, which previously had not been at all united, rallied in the face of the intervention, and announced a *jihad*—a holy war against the unfaithful. They recruited all Afghans who remained faithful to Islam and to their motherland to their holy cause.

All antigovernment factions joined the struggle, not only contrary to the PDPA regime, but especially against the invading strangers. The irreconcilable opposition became in essence a state within a state.

The Afghan resistance was not monolithic politically; it embraced different groups, from supporters of the monarchy to left-leaning radicals. From information obtained from various sources, in the early 1980s there were as many as a hundred various factions operating at one time or another against the government. But there were six major groupings.

The Islamic Party of Afghanistan (IPA) was organized in 1976 as the result of the merging of several different groups, with an ultraright-wing orientation within the Afghan branch of the international organization The Moslem Brotherhood, and its young men who were members of the Moslem Youth organization. The ruling body of the IPA was its executive committee, with a headquarters in Peshawar and a liaison office in Iran.

The executive committee consisted of the leaders of seven functional subcommittees—military, cultural, propaganda, finance, administration, information, and legal. It directed the activities of provincial committees that in turn coordinated the actions of regional, district, and small rural subcommittees.

The military committee was called the Main Military Command of the IPA and Headquarters for Operational Leadership. It commanded and coordinated military missions of armed counterrevolutionary formations in Afghanistan.

The IPA spread its party program widely, dealing with such notions as revolution and personality from the Islamic point of view. Under the program, the IPA's main goal was the overthrow of the government's rule, which would, in turn, restore some traditional Islamic ways of life: *purdah* (a veil worn by Moslem women), separate schools for boys and girls, use of a national uniform for officials instead of western clothes, and a ban on alcohol and gambling. If these programs were implemented, western influence would be greatly reduced, and something like the present-day fundamentalist regime in Iran would be instituted.

New recruits joining the IPA had to be recommended by at least one party member and pay an initiation fee of 500 afghani. In a ceremony, people joining the party took an oath on the holy Koran, promising to be faithful to the cause of Islam. If the oath was broken, the punishment was death.

The official publication of the IPA was the newspaper *Shahadat* ("death for belief"). A special committee on propaganda was organized, with a mobile radio station at its disposal as well as many ways to disseminate information in Pushtu and Dari.

The leader of the IPA was Gulbuddin Hikmatiyar, one of the most influential leaders of the opposition. He was born in 1944 in the Imam-Sahib district of Kunduz Province son of a rich landowner. In 1970 he entered Kabul University, specializing in engineering.

Even at that time, he advocated strict observance of Islam and stood in opposition to the regime. He was an activist and later was the leader of the Afghan branch of The Moslem Brotherhood. In 1972, under the rule of King Zahir Shah, he was arrested for the militant stand he took on the ideas of Islamic rebirth.

After the overthrow of the monarchy, he was released and immediately began to agitate against M. Daud, whose rule Hikmatiyar called "corrupt and anti-Islamic." In 1976, he founded his own party and two years later he organized militant uprisings against Daud's short-lived government in the provinces of Parwan, Laghman, and Uruzgan. The rebellion was suppressed, however, and he had to flee to Pakistan.

After the April revolution in Afghanistan, Hikmatiyar continued his pro-Islamic struggle against the new government. But soon he and the new president, Amin, agreed to cease their confrontation and to try to collaborate. Hikmatiyar was to become prime minister. But this friendship was short-lived when, in still another coup, Amin was overthrown by Babrak Karmal* and Gulbuddin declared a *jihad* against the Babrak Karmal government.

---

*Amin reportedly was killed by a Soviet Spetsnaz team in conjunction with invading forces of the Soviet Union.

Gulbuddin claimed to be the leader of all the opposition forces, and step by step he approached this goal as he tried to spread his influence wider. He was active in the provinces of Kabul, Nangarhar, Kunar, Logar, Kunduz, and Badakhshan.

The Islamic Society of Afghanistan (ISA) was founded in 1976 by those who had been close to the former king, Zahir-Shah, and who at this time were living in Pakistan. The aim of this faction, as it was put in numerous appeals, was to "wage armed struggle against Daud and Russian imperialism in Afghanistan."

The ISA did not accept the April revolution of 1978, and under the slogan of Islamic justice it began the struggle of creating in Afghanistan an Islamic republic. The members of the organization were mullahs, landowners, bureaucrats, and other people who were followers of Islam.

The ISA's headquarters was in Pakistan, and like the IPA also had offices in Iran. The organization owned a wide network of propaganda means, especially newspapers such as *Kalbe Osie* ("heart of Asia") and *Mujahid* ("fighter for belief"), and a magazine, *Misak-a Hun* ("drop of blood"). The ISA also had significant military forces and a network of Islamic committees.

The majority of ISA members were Hazaras and Tadzhiks by nationality, the most backward parts of the population in the past. The ISA was active in Hazarajat, in the provinces of Herat, Farah, Ghor, Badghis, Bamian, and certain other parts of the country where Tadzhiks and Hazaras lived.

The ISA head is Burhanuddin Rabbani, born in 1940 in the province of Badakhshan. He graduated from Kabul University, where he studied Islamic law. He later continued his education in Egypt and received the degree of doctor of theology. Before the April revolution of 1978, Rabbani owned large farms in Kabul and Nangarhar.

The National Front of Islamic Revolution of Afghanistan (NFIRA) was founded in Pakistan in 1978. It proclaimed its goal to be the defender of Islam in Afghanistan. The NFIRA is most closely connected with the United States. It worked in close contact with the anti-Soviet National Labor Council in Europe (which has branches in West Germany and Belgium) and spread leaflets in Afghanistan, printed in Russian, to undermine the morale of Soviet soldiers while they were stationed in Afghanistan.

A man joining NFIRA solemnly promised "to sacrifice all my belongings and my life itself in the struggle for raising the word of Allah, glorifying Islam, and liberating the country."

The NFIRA's military detachments were active in Ghazni, Paktika, Zabul, and Kabul. Said Ahmad Gailani was NFIRA's leader. His religious orientation did not conceal his ambition for power. He came from an influential feudal clan that owned a great amount of land in various regions of Afghanistan. He is known for his ties with the royal family because his wife is the granddaughter of the former king.

Gailani was the descendant of Iraqis who were influential members of the Sufi Order of Cadiri. He would later become the leader of this order, with a spiritual title of *pir*. He is revered by other members of his sect as the descendant of the prophet Muhammed. The majority of his supporters were former rich landowners and state officials, who call him Effandi Jan Agha.

Traditionally, members of the Gailani clan are spiritual tutors in Pushtun tribes in the province of Paktia. Before the April revolution, Gailani was more of a businessman than an ecclesiastic. He was the dealer for Peugeot automobiles in Kabul and owned considerable land in Jalalabad. In December 1978, after the confiscation of his property, he emigrated to Pakistan, where he began an active struggle against the new regime. Gailani claimed to be the father of all the Mujahidin.

His closest associate was Zia Nasseri, who claims to be "Gailani's personal representative" and even "head of the National Front." He came from a rich Afghan family, the son of a prominent intelligence operative in the king's inner circle. He became an American citizen and was educated in the United States.

The Islamic Revolution Movement of Afghanistan (IRMA) was founded in June 1978 in Pakistan by members of a rightist Islamic organization, Servants of the Koran. This group was organized several years before the April revolution of 1978 by Ibrahim Mojaddedi, a religious figure descended from the well-known clan of Mojaddedi *hazrats* (religious leaders) headed by *mawlawi* Muhammed Nabi (Muhammadi) whose roots traditionally go back to the Khalif Omar, an associate of the prophet Muhammed. At the time of the Soviet intervention, the group was headed by moulawi Muhammed Nabi (Muhammadi).

The central headquarters of IRMA was located in Peshawar and, like the others, had offices in Iran. The headquarters consisted of several departments: military, political, cultural activities, counterintelligence, emigration, and finance.

IRMA's program goals were very much like those of the IPA. It was put forward as an appeal to Afghan Moslems and was titled "What Do We Want?" Their program contained twenty-one points, including declaring *jihad* against elements hostile to Islam, creating a truly Islamic Republic of Afghanistan, and defending the rights of Islamic minorities in non-Moslem countries.

As a rule, those who joined the organization were mullahs dissatisfied with the April revolution, various fanatically religious young people, and former officials and common people who hoped to achieve freedom and the good life.

Armed fighters of the group are known for their brutal tactics, which caused some Islamic opposition parties to condemn their actions. In particular, G. Hikmatiyar has said that IRMA "profaned Islam."

IRMA spreads its ideas through the newspapers *Hedayat-e Islam* ("leadership of Islam") and *Al Muslimin* ("Moslems") and by the use of leaflets, posters, and mailing lists. It acts mainly in the northern parts of the country, as well as in the provinces of Ghazni, Kabul, Paktia, Herat, Kandahar, Helmand, and Farah.

IRMA's leader, M. Nabi, was born in 1937. He was schooled in Islamic theology and could be classified as an Orthodox Moslem. He actively participated in the work of the faction called Moslem Brotherhood. In 1973 he was arrested for writing and publishing antigovernment religious poems. After the April revolution of 1978, he emigrated to Pakistan, where he instigated an armed struggle against the government, becoming most active after the overthrow of President Amin.

The Front of National Liberation of Afghanistan (FNLA) was founded in June 1978 using as a basis eight groups of émigrés existing since the 1970s who were known as "fervent Moslems." The goals of the FNLA were creating an Islamic society based on justice and equality and democratic traditions; observing principles of Islamic fraternity; defending the country's independence, culture, history, national honor, and dignity; defending truly Islamic traditions and moral values; and liberating the Afghan people from neocolonialism, atheism, and Marxism.

The FNLA declared a *jihad* against the government of Afghanistan with the aim of overthrowing it and creating Islamic rule, where all political, economic, and public affairs would be based on Islam, and personal and public freedom would be guaranteed. In all propaganda of the front, its members call themselves *"Mujahidin* of the way of the truth." The FNLA publishes the *Wahdat* ("unity") newspaper, which is printed in Western Europe.

The front is supported by the former king and his associates and is especially influential in the regions where Pushtuns lived and in northern, eastern, and southeastern provinces.

The leader of the FNLA, Sebghatullah Mojaddedi, was born in 1926. His ancestry includes many well-known religious figures who controlled charitable endeavors in Afghanistan before the April revolution. Mojaddedi received the highest level theological education and is well-known in the Moslem world.

Mojaddedi became the most ardent foe of even the slightest reforms implemented in Afghanistan under the king. During the period 1968–1971 this conservative leader sharply criticized Zahir Shah. Daud had him arrested and jailed for five years. In 1978 he emigrated to Pakistan and started actively to instigate warfare against the leftist regime in Afghanistan. On May 12, 1979 his Peshawar headquarters published a call to Afghans to wage a *jihad* (holy war) against the "Godless Communist regime in Kabul."

Sebghatullah Mojaddedi was one of the most prominent figures in the leadership of the Afghan branch of the Moslem Brotherhood and of its special faction for young people, Moslem Youth. But, after the split of the Afghan branch of the Moslem Brotherhood—when Gulbuddin Hikmatiyar founded the IPA—Mojaddedi founded and headed the Society of Moslem Theologians (*Jamiat-e-Ulema*).

The Islamic Party of Afghanistan-Khales was founded in 1979 as the result of the split of the party of the same name previously organized by G. Hikmatiyar. It was headed by Muhammed Yunus who was nicknamed Khales ("pious"), a former associate and ally of Hikmatiyar. Their split was caused by different views on cooperating with other opposition organizations in their mutual struggle against the government.

Khales, who advocated unification, sharply criticized Gulbuddin Hikmatiyar, who had demanded that all opposition forces should come under the IPA, and report personally to him.

In fact, the IPA-Khales program, social composition, and structure did not differ particularly from those of Hikmatiyar's basic party. His breakaway program was particularly influential in the provinces of Nangarhar, Paktia, and Logar.

In June 1980, the Islamic Union for Liberation of Afghanistan (ICLA) was founded. It was especially important, because it comprised five of the most influential opposition organizations: the ISA, NFIRA, IRMA, FNLA, and IPA-Khales. The Supreme Council of the ICLA was instituted and headed by B. Rabbani. The ICLA proclaimed as its main goals the liberation of Afghanistan from atheism and Communism and formation of an Afghan government on the basis of the Koran and Sunna, and cooperation with all Islamic movements fighting for the liberation of Moslem land. In April 1981, however, the union was disbanded because its operations did not contribute enough to the progress of the holy war in Afghanistan.

On June 3, 1981, the formation of the Islamic Union of Mujahidin of Afghanistan (IUMA) was announced in Islamabad. It had a similar composition to the ICLA and comprised several of the same factions: the ISA, IPA, IRMA, FNLA, and IPA-Khales. The elected leader of the IUMA was Abdurassul Saiyaf, a well-known theologian who had been educated in Afghanistan and Egypt. He was especially active in disseminating propaganda of the ideas of Moslem Brotherhood to the youth. In 1973, after the overthrow of Zahir Shah, Saiyaf was arrested and jailed. After he was finally freed in 1980, he immediately emigrated to Pakistan.

At the end of 1981, the heads of the organizations united in IUMA signed a charter that provided for active participation of representatives of all organizations and "respected religious authorities." Under the charter, the Supreme Council of IUMA was created. It was to form the Afghan Interim Government and formulate a constitution based on the principles of the religion. But this organization also did not last long. The individual authorities were having trouble in uniting under any umbrella organization, a situation that plagues them to the present day.

The promonarchist wing of IUMA (composed of NFIRA, IRMA, and FNLA) proposed as their leader the former king, Zahir Shah. G. Hikmatiyar was categorically against it, arguing that Zahir Shah was "a traitor who opened to the Communists the way to Afghanistan." Because of this, he "was and remains IPA's enemy."

This split of the council resulted in the creation of a new Islamic Council of Mujahidin of Afghanistan, composed of different members. In September 1981 in Quetta, a conference was held of the leaders of three of the groups mentioned above (NFIRA, IRMA, and FNLA), former members of the royal government and parliament, and influential tribal leaders from regions near the borders.

At this conference, it was agreed that M. Zahir Shah would be declared the leader of the entire opposition movement. Major General Abdul Wali (son-in-law of the former king and former commander of the Central Corps of the Afghan armed forces) was appointed as the immediate operating executive for the new leader of the opposition.

In their turn, leaders of the IPA, ISA, and IPA-Khales agreed to create a new union of other parties with the participation of groups headed by N. Mansur and M. M. Logari which had separated themselves from IRMA and FNLA. In February 1982 an official announcement was made about creating the United Front ("Jabhe-a Mottahid") headed by ISA leader B. Rabbani. Gulbuddin Hikmatiyar was elected his deputy. In this way, the opposition forces were split into two competing camps—the monarchists and the Islamic republicans.

At a meeting on March 4, 1982, in Peshawar that was organized by the supporters of the United Front, Zahir Shah and his associates were condemned as the "unfaithful." And on the same day, supporters of the former king attacked the office of B. Rabbani.

The primary reason for unification and, paradoxically, at the same time, the main reason for dissension in the opposition camp is the same principle of national-ethnic unity. The American magazine *Newsweek* wrote that rebels of different ethnic groups in the blaze of nationalism are also involved in deadly animosity and that religious figures of different nationalities are making the common struggle weaker.[1]

At various times in some provinces, deadly combat took place between armed detachments of parties with different national-ethnic orientation. Both the Afghan and western press frequently reported such clashes.

So there was really no stable organization among the forces of the Afghan opposition that could form a truly united front against the Afghan government. Their unification and therefore their successes were hampered by the significant differences among the opposition groups. They had continuous trouble in dealing with a variety of questions on how to conduct the antigovernment struggle and how to achieve their ultimate goals.

Groups of rebels, who were trying to strengthen their positions in regions under their control, found there that "Islamic committees" were functioning as temporary bases of political power. The tasks of these committees were to establish and maintain military and administrative control, distribute armaments from abroad, spread written propaganda such as leaflets and posters, collect taxes, and recruit local people into military detachments.

The opposition forces were able to operate in their warfare with government forces only when the strength of the armed detachments, which differed in composition, level of readiness, and equipment, was sufficient to match that of their opponents. The foreign press sources reported that "the number of armed rebels is from 40,000 to 100,000 men."[2]

It is obvious that, without foreign help and support, it would have been impossible for the Mujahidin to plan for and conduct long-term and significant combat activities. They have received support in impressive quantities. "Large-scale and prolonged guerrilla activities," wrote an Indian researcher, "demand huge resources and the rebels could never have such resources available without help from abroad."[3]

But from American sources, this help at least until 1979 was limited to humanitarian aid. For instance, congressional aide John B. Ritch, who traveled officially to Pakistan in 1984 and "unofficially" to Afghanistan, wrote in his report to the Senate Committee on Foreign Relations: "During the first phase . . . of the revolution, American involvement was limited to supplying the Mujahidin with medical equipment and medicine. . . ."[4] We hardly believe, nevertheless, that the fundamental policy of the USA toward Afghanistan was to be limited to shipments of medicine. A French editorialist speculated:

> There are no grounds to believe that having lost Iran, the U.S. will give up its influence in the region. . . . The U.S. wishes to use events in the Middle East as a lever to cause the various countries there to be hostile towards the USSR. . . . This is the goal of the U.S., and to achieve it, the United States is providing all possible support to this rebellion. An agreement with Pakistan is necessary for this, and there are favorable conditions present to obtain such an arrangement.[5]

Speaking of favorable conditions, the French newspaper *Figaro* may have had in mind, in particular, the visit by U.S. Vice Secretary of State W. Christopher to Pakistan in the spring of 1979. Specific questions on the level of aid to the Afghan rebels were discussed during his trip. These same questions were discussed during a visit to Islamabad in August 1979 by a U.S. congressional delegation, members of which met with commanders of Afghan armed formations that were acting from the territory of Pakistan against government forces.

In 1973, after the antimonarchist coup by M. Daud, the United States founded in the vicinity of Attoka in Pakistan a training center for Afghan "potential guerrillas," which was commanded by G. Hikmatiyar.[6] The greatest support in maintaining that center and the arming and training of combat groups of Afghan fundamentalists was provided by Pakistani leadership. Other secret services and support came from the fundamentalist Jamiat-e Islami and Arab Moslem Brotherhood. After fruitless attempts to organize antigovernment rebellions by peasants in various provinces of Afghanistan, many Afghan fundamentalist combat groups went to Pakistan. Those who remained continued their active hostile actions in Afghanistan. Receiving financial support from abroad, they were able to create, in several cities of Afghanistan, broad networks of underground groups. They sought to involve students, low-level officials, and the military, as well as merchants and craftsmen. They established secret chains of agents, caches of arms, and underground printing presses, getting themselves ready for a new attempt at an armed coup in the country. By the date of the revolution of 1978, these organizations had already established a bridgehead in Pakistan and a network of underground cells in the cities at their disposal. Only two weeks after the April revolution began, detachments of Afghan insurgents, trained and armed thanks to donations by international organizations, started to arrive illegally in Afghanistan.[7]

"Should the U.S. arm the insurgents?" asks Anthony Arnold, who was first secretary of the U.S. Embassy in Afghanistan (1974-76) in his book written after the Soviet invasion. "In any case, the Afghans will continue to fight even with stones, if need be, and we should not deny them the chance to be more effective. . . ."[8]

After the April revolution of 1978 in Afghanistan, much attention was paid in the United States to the opposition forces. With the appearance of the first refugees from Afghanistan, different American private and charitable organizations became interested. Funds such as the Aid to Afghanistan Committee, the Asia Society, financed by the Rockefeller family, the Organization of Asia Fund, and the American Drug Enforcement Agency (DEA) provided help to the refugees and armed soldiers in Pakistan near the borders of Afghanistan.[9]

Arab countries were also involved as they followed their traditions and actively supported the Afghan opposition. For example, in October 1979, the U.S. ambassador to Saudi Arabia, who was a specialist in Arab affairs, was told by an official of that country, Ash-Shura, that initially the government of Saudi Arabia withheld financial aid to Afghan resistance forces headed by S. Mojaddedi and S. A. Gailani, hoping that "this would move them to create a more effective front." But later, emphasized Ash-Shura, the government decided that it was necessary to help the Afghan opposition, even if Mojaddedi and Gailani failed to agree with each other. As Ash-Shura put it, the aim of the Saudi Arabian government was not to allow the rebels to grow weaker and thus change the balance of forces.[10]

Until January 1980 the United States and other countries continued to conceal the true scale of their financial and other aid to Afghan forces opposing the government. "A complete picture of travel routes of the aid and the quantities of arms and ammunition were not available, even to well-informed intelligence services."[11]

At the same time, judging by the information available, official circles in the United States were not yet certain about the events in Afghanistan, although their sympathy generally went to the opposition. For instance, an American representative in Afghanistan, J. B. Amstutz, reported to Washington his perception of the situation:

A victory by the opposition will have double consequences for the United States, but if we consider properly all the pros and cons it will be clear that such a victory will be in the interests of the United States. . . . The regime which will be established by the opposition if they are victorious apparently will not include in the list of their immediate tasks, social and economic reforms so necessary for this backward country. It is quite possible that opposition forces will begin to avenge themselves in order to settle the score with traditional enemies. This will be bad for the reputation of a new, post-PDPA, regime in the sphere of human rights. . . . Still, it will be in our interests that the government of Taraki and Amin should vanish, despite future obstacles for social and economic reforms in Afghanistan.[12]

Newsweek magazine wrote that among members of the Carter administration there were discussions about the covert intervention of the U.S. and civil war between the rebels and Taraki's regime.[13]

If before the Soviet invasion of Afghanistan shipments of military goods to Afghanistan from the United States, Pakistan, Iran, Saudi Arabia, and other countries were not made public, after that intervention, this aid was openly discussed, and gained new scale and character. "We must provide direct support to nationalist and rebellious forces in Afghanistan. We should directly help Pakistan with arms," Senator Charles Percy stated in a speech in the Senate in January 1980.[14]

In January 1980, the United States admitted that it was supplying the Afghan opposition forces with arms in connection with a covert program of the Central Intelligence Agency (CIA).[15]

In February 1980, the American press reported that the CIA had begun covert actions to supply the Afghan rebels with weapons. The plan of the operation was endorsed by a special coordinating committee with National Security Advisor Zbigniew Brzezinski as chairman; it was approved by President Carter himself. Wrote Indian researcher Bhabani Sen Gupta:

> This was the major CIA operation after the one in Angola in 1975. The rebels fought with light field weapons of Soviet design shipped from Egypt and China. . . . Weapons were also delivered by Pakistan. It was reported that Iran also provided the rebels with numbers of weapons. Egypt announced that rebellious groups were trained in Egypt and then sent back with weapons . . . . China also sent arms by way of the Karakorum Highway.[16]

It is evident that of all the nations supporting the rebels, the most effective aid came from the United States and Pakistan, with its common border with Afghanistan. Pakistan was especially interested in establishing a friendly regime with its neighbor as opposed to one dominated by the Soviet Union. An article in an official Indian weekly reported that the Afghan guerrillas and their allies were making use of Pakistani territory for organizing a holy war against the incumbent Afghan government. The article stated that Peter Bensinger, head of the DEA in Washington, sent a letter to the U.S. ambassador in Pakistan that clearly showed that Pakistani territory was not only used for training Afghan rebels but also was placed at the full disposal of the American CIA.

The letter informed the U.S. ambassador in Islamabad that "Lewis Adams, special agent, head of the DEA office in Lahore, left for Peshawar" and mentioned that it was he who had organized and carried out an operation on January 18, 1979 in Lahore, the results of which turned out especially useful for American interests.

Though Lewis Adams was known officially as the head of the Lahore office of the DEA, he had been purposely sent to Pakistan in 1977 with the mission of helping the Pakistani secret service to organize various intelligence operations. But the very action for which he was praised by Bensinger in his letter was the meeting of the commanders of Afghan insurgent forces on January 18, 1980. Later, Adams organized such meetings in other cities of Pakistan as well.

The essence of the above-mentioned letter and the action it perpetrated were in every detail described to a correspondent from *Blitz* weekly by a former official from the DEA. For quite understandable reasons this person wishes to remain anonymous. He did not offer any conclusions but disclosed various actions and dates that clarify the picture of a CIA plan to make ready their broad support for the *jihad,* mainly from the territory of Pakistan. The magazine continued that in connection with the assassination of the U.S. ambassador to Afghanistan, Adolph Dubs, which happened in Kabul on February 14, 1979, Washington held Taraki's regime responsible. All agreements on economic aid to Afghanistan were canceled. No substitute for Dubs was sent to Kabul because the Americans had already begun to accuse the Afghan government of human rights violations.

After the Soviet invasion, Pakistan began to receive military and economic aid from the United States in the amount of about $400 million. But within this secret agreement between the two countries, a portion of this sum was set apart to subsidize covert military actions against the government of Afghanistan.

Blitz cites a report of the Swiss daily newspaper *Neue Zürcher Zeitung,* in February 1979, which categorically asserted that the military rulers of Pakistan, without any publicity, granted the rebels about 20 million rupees. The news story goes on to say that the source of the money was the CIA, and that all the money would be spent by the rebels for arms.

Blitz also reports that in June 1978, a senior official of the Strategic and International Research Center of Georgetown University, closely connected with the intelligence community of the United States, wrote that:

. . . taking into consideration America's obvious interest in security and stability in this region, it would be useful for the U.S.

government to consult with Iran and Pakistan and cooperate with them. A calm, but noticeable demonstration of understanding of their concerns would placate them and at the same time serve as an indirect warning in case the new government [Taraki's regime] tried to create complications for its neighbors. In reality everything was the opposite of this. These same neighbors were busily creating complications for Afghanistan and were interfering in this country's affairs.[17]

American and Pakistani actions in support of the Afghan rebel forces were also covered by the Lebanese press. For example, the *Ash-Shaab* newspaper, citing western journalists, wrote that, acting on American guidance, Afghan opposition leaders began forming an Afghan government in exile in Pakistan that officially would be called the Revolutionary People's Council of Afghanistan. Members of this shadow government would be Gulbuddin Hikmatiyar, Said Ahmad Gailani, Zia Nasseri, and Bashir Zakria, an Afghan opposition leader then living in New York.

As the Americans planned, this government would eventually request military aid from Pakistan to liberate Afghanistan. Thus, Pakistan and the United States, supporting the government in exile, would have a ready pretext for immediate interference in the affairs of Afghanistan.

As a part of this support, Pakistani armed forces units had already begun training in approved methods of combat in regions close to the Afghan border. At the same time, the Americans were trying hard to persuade various Third World countries to support the "Afghan government in exile" and to ensure its being acknowledged by the United Nations.[18]

Dwelling on the same topic, the Lebanese weekly *Al-Kifah al-Arabi* pointed out that the CIA was using Moslem extremist groups such as the Moslem–Brotherhood for hostile activities against Afghanistan and Iran.[19]

It is important to emphasize that the sympathies of the United States, Pakistan, and other countries were pointed toward providing both military and humanitarian aid to the Afghan opposition. Although earlier, the aid was mainly humanitarian, these countries became determined after the Soviet invasion to step up military support. In the early days, however, the American press was somewhat reserved about it. For example, the *Washington Post,* reflecting opinion in well-informed circles, wrote critically that the United States had shipped weapons to opposition detachments involved in combat in Afghanistan. These weapons, wrote the newspaper, were directed across the border of Pakistan with Afghanistan, which was 1,400 miles long, running across mountains. The shipments were mainly comprised of small arms and relatively simple types of antitank weapons that would give a fighter the ability to destroy armored vehicles. The American shipments began after December 24, but were not particularly extensive then. They reflect the Carter administration's decision to try to help encircled detachments of rebels that were inferior to the enemy in terms of weaponry.

Although it was not known in detail how these arms were shipped, they were probably brought together by the Central Intelligence Agency. Main congressional committees that kept covert operations under surveillance were constantly informed by the State Department and the CIA about these actions of the government.

The decision to send arms, though in relatively small quantities, was a tactic that significantly added to the aid that the United States had already secretly provided to Afghan rebels in the months before the Soviet invasion. It had been limited to small amounts of medicine and communication equipment sent to scattered rebellious tribes. The Americans also gave advice and recommendations to the rebels about where they could buy weapons themselves.

China also intensified its efforts to help the Mujahidin, mainly through Pakistan. "The Chinese, judging by available information, are ready to sell to Islamabad light tanks and other types of equipment," the British newspaper *The Guardian* reported on January 19, 1980.

This same topic concerned the *Daily Telegraph* on the same date as it informed its readers: "Pakistan has concentrated seven divisions on the border with Afghanistan and China also has its troops in its sector of the border and is sending large amounts of military equipment to Pakistan by way of the Karakorum highway."

From the *Tokyo Shimbun* of January 23, 1980:

> At meetings with Pakistani leadership, Chinese minister for Foreign Affairs Huan Hua expressed his opinion that the situation in Afghanistan posed a "serious threat" for Pakistan and prom-

ised new economic and military aid to the country. China presented to Pakistan a list of weapons it was prepared to supply and is going to satisfy any demands of Islamabad.

The United States most willingly cooperated with China in the plan of providing support to the Mujahidin. This idea was expressed in a speech by American Defense Secretary Harold Brown at a press conference at the San Diego Naval Air Station in January 1980. He remarked that the United States and China were going to undertake parallel actions in the Middle East and among them to help Pakistan. "For us," emphasized Mr. Brown, "strengthening the American presence in this region will be very important and we will undertake extraordinary measures for this region of Central Asia."

The American television network NBC reported on January 7, 1980, that while in Beijing, U.S. Defense Secretary Brown, in his toast at a banquet, condemned Soviet policy toward Afghanistan in strong terms and underlined the necessity of broadening military contacts between China and the United States. For the first time in history, a senior American official spoke publicly about the possibility of a military alliance between the United States and China.

Such statements were well received in Pakistan and in all the Afghan resistance groups. But in some other countries, especially in India, such a military alliance aroused grave concerns. In her interview with the American network ABC in 1980, Indian Prime Minister Indira Gandhi said that the United States is implementing a global strategy to aid the Afghan insurgents, some of whom are working closely with China to arm Pakistan, thus representing a real threat to India.

As a result, demonstrating policies of the Carter administration, the Afghan rebels began to receive military aid on a growing scale and of the most modern type. Ronald Reagan, as a presidential candidate in March 1980, disclosed his intention to help the Afghan opposition. Similar declarations were made by China, Egypt, Saudi Arabia, and a number of other countries. These were not mere words. Before the Soviet invasion, the Mujahidin were armed mainly with outdated British rifles and less often with Soviet AK-47 assault rifles; after the beginning of 1980 and the Soviet invasion, they received growing numbers of weapons such as 82mm mortars and 75mm recoilless guns; Chinese versions of light air-defense weapons, such as the ZPY-2 and SAM-7 air-defense missiles; portable RPG-7 antitank grenade launchers from Egypt; AK-47 and AKM assault rifles; and great numbers of antitank mines, mainly of Chinese and Italian production.[20]

Between 1980 and 1984, the CIA provided $325 million as military aid to the Mujahidin; in 1984 they planned to spend another $250 million to support the Afghan opposition.[21] American officials, however, differed in their statements as to the amount of military aid that would be given to Afghan resistance forces, saying that it amounted to only $208 million, twice as much as the United States spent in 1984.[22] To confuse the situation even further, another source said that U.S. government aid in 1980–1984 amounted to $625 million.[23] Keeping up the trend, in 1986, military aid to forces countering the Afghan government and Soviet troops amounted to $470 million. Whatever the correct total, the amount of aid provided was certainly substantial.

Rather impressive also were donations from other countries. For example, in 1983, according to the *Arab News,* September 9, 1985, Saudi Arabia, China, and Israel supplied combat vehicles and weapons worth U.S. $100 million; in 1985 Saudi Arabia alone provided $200 million for similar armaments.

When on September 14, 1985 an *Arab News* correspondent asked Pakistani President Zia ul-Haq in Jidda how useful he thought the aid to Afghanistan was from Islamic countries as well as the West and China, and if he had any dissatisfactions, Gen. Zia answered: "No. We are thankful to all of them for their being consistent—Moslem countries, China and western states."

The Moslem Brotherhood—and its affiliated Moslem Youth—is a fanatical far right organization. Its aim is an uncompromising struggle against the forces of the left and its ultimate defeat. In July 1975 they formed a group plotting to overthrow the republican government and set up an Islamic state. Strangely enough, it was joined in this plot by a far left extremist group with a Maoist orientation, *Sholay-e-Jaweid.* Its slogan was "The Rifle Brings Power." *Sholay-e-Jaweid* did not have a clearly stated platform. Instead, its aim was to sow confusion and fight for power, causing it to back any organization attempting to overthrow the government. On the other hand, the Moslem Brotherhood had a clear-cut goal of establishing a government thoroughly based on the Islamic religion. It was supported by many of the more wealthy landowners and businessmen, as well as senior Moslem theologians.

The aid that the Afghan opposition received was not limited to that provided by the United States and other countries through government channels. Help from various funds, private parties, and organizations was also sent to the Mujahidin. Direct and significant financial support to fundamentalist organizations in Afghanistan was furnished by the Jamiat-e-Islami of Pakistan. Through this society, aid was directed from the Arab Moslem Brotherhood and other fundamentalist organizations of Arab countries.* For example, a Saudi committee that collected money for the Afghan opposition in 1984 offered to the fundamentalist leadership of the Islamic Union of Mujahidin of Afghanistan (IUMA-7) 52 million Saudi riyals, which is equal to U.S. $15 million. In Pakistan the committee also bought and gave to IUMA-7 material and equipment worth 38 million Saudi riyals.

A partial list of equipment given to the rebels in 1984, and made available both to the Mujahidin and their families living in camps controlled by IUMA, includes 35,000 tents, 14 by 14 meters; 100 tents for schools and mosques, 20 by 10 meters; clothing for 230,000 men, women, and children; 388,000 pairs of shoes for men, women, and children; 629,000 socks; 46,600 blankets; 200,000 sets of underwear; 160,000 headgear; and 8,000 sacks (100 kilograms each) of rice. Apart from these goods, the committee paid for the building of several mosques, drilled several wells, constructed 22 schools, and bought in Pakistan medical equipment and medicine worth 21 million Pakistani rupees.[24]

But military aid was far more extensive than the humanitarian variety. In 1986, Pakistan and the United States agreed that over a period of

---

*As a kind of coordinator for the several opposition groups, an Afghan committee was set up in 1980 without the Islamic Conference Organization, a body that met regularly. Among the groups coordinated were *Hezb-e-Islami,* led by Gulbuddin Hikmatiyar; *Jamiat-e-Islami,* led by Professor Burhanuddin Rabbani; and *Harakat-e-Islami,* led by Muhammed Nabi Muhammadi. These three organizations do not differ much. Only their ambitions and their leaders' overall positions of importance are somewhat different, with the leaders' roles bending to change over the years. While Soviet troops were in-country, they were united in combat actions against the foreign invaders. They also agreed on the deposition of Najibullah as a precondition to peace talks. Their views on the future of Afghanistan are different, however. The *Jamiat-e-Islami* champions a war to its triumphal end, having a position close to that of the Moslem Brotherhood. Hikmatiyar wants to create a fundamentalist religious state with close ties to Pakistan and Iran. Rabbani is a more moderate politician who favors setting up a broadly based opposition.

five years, the Pakistani armed forces would be provided armaments worth more than $4 billion. A portion of this aid was to be given to the Afghan insurgents, although Pakistani Foreign Minister Z. Nurani denied this report.

A significant part of American military support was sent to the rebels through other countries in order to equip its detachments with modern weapons. The United States could not provide direct support to the Mujahidin militarily and financially because of moral considerations. For example, IUMA-7's position about accepting foreign aid was clear and uncompromised until June 1986. The Afghan fundamentalist opposition was not willing to accept American and other western aid in any form, since it would be contrary to the main strategic principle of "Neither East, nor West." In this regard, IPA's leader G. Hikmatiyar, speaking in February 1980 in Teheran before foreign journalists, said:

> We do not wish our country to be turned into an arena for war between two superpowers like Vietnam. We are fighting for a free, independent and Moslem Afghanistan . . . and we will accept aid only from those who share our goals and agree with them. . . . As far as the U.S. and other allied countries are concerned, the fact is that they not only do not help and cannot help our Islamic movement in Afghanistan but their interference in the affairs of the Afghan revolution serves only to destroy the pure character of the Islamic movement. . . . Iran is the only country that can support the Islamic revolution in Afghanistan more acceptably than any other country.[25]

The official publication of IUMA-7, the *Kiyam-e-Hak* magazine, in 1985 published an article by Dr. Muhammad Zahir Sadik in which foreign aid was discussed as follows:

> . . . some forces stand as supporters of our jihad, but instead it works to the profit of red imperialism. For example, they say that the CIA helps us in our struggle. The BBC announced that this intelligence organization assigned $250 million to help us, or 80 percent of its annual budget for operations worldwide. We do not deny the fact that some freedom-loving countries help our emigrants. We do not deny the fact that Islamic and humanitarian

organizations help to treat Mujahidin wounds. We do not deny the fact that the Mujahidin and refugees receive their share of food, clothing, and medicine. But we say proudly that we are waging our struggle by ourselves. . . . Publication of other such information is a great blow to our *jihad,* insulting the blood of our *shahids.*[26]

However, on more solid ground, from the point of view of funda-mentalist Islam, the foreword to a Teheran-published book, *Papers of a Spy Nest,* stated that:

Americans try to portray the Afghan Moslems' movement . . . as a pro-American struggle. . . . This leads nonaligned countries and liberation movements to stop providing aid. As a result Afghan rebels became convinced that the U.S. and their allies adhere to freedom and independence. American aid is in some cases channeled through countries that are allies of the U.S., such as Saudi Arabia, Egypt, and Pakistan, so that Afghan rebels are beginning to be-lieve that these are truly Moslem countries and wish that Afghanistan were ruled by such Moslems. This belief leads to the acceptance of this American penetration into the fighting Afghan troops as normal and natural. . . .[27]

Because of these fundamentalist principles, IUMA-7 had so far refused to accept assistance from the United States and other western coun-tries as well as Arab countries thought to be not Moslem enough. The IUMA-7 leaders made no mention of Chinese aid.

At first glance, it appears that the inter-Arab organizations such as Moslem Brotherhood, with its various committees and funds attached to it, and the Jamiat-e-Islami of Pakistan and other nongovernment fundamentalist alliances were the major supporters of the Afghan fundamentalists. At least, the Afghan fundamentalists themselves stated clearly that they obtained help from these sources. At the same time, it was also quite obvious that such support could not be in sufficient quantity if the Mujahidin were to survive and wage an armed struggle. But if they had admitted the truth publicly, they would have ruined their reputation as an independent and purely Islamic force. In reality their "illegal" financial aid came largely from the United States, Saudi Arabia, and Pakistan.

However, it is worth mentioning that there was no unanimity within IUMA itself on the issue of western help. G. Hikmatiyar was totally opposed to any U.S. support, whereas A. R. Saiyaf and U. Kales admitted that they could not do without it. They insisted that it should be unconditional.[28] B. Rabbani also moved away from the position of his IUMA-7 ally, G. Hikmatiyar, on the issue.

Another faction within the fundamentalist camp, IUMA-3, as a prowestern alliance, tried to get support from any source. Two of its leaders, S. Mojaddedi and S. A. Gailani, were well known in American and West German political circles. They had visited both countries and were well acquainted with the western life-style. Officials in the west found their political outlook and the goals they set attractive. These leaders, as well as M. Nabi Muhammadi, also kept in touch with the top officials of Saudi Arabia, Kuwait, and Egypt, and with Moslem leaders of other Arab states.

As we have seen, there was no unity within the Afghan opposition. Rival factions fought with each other to keep their existing sources of help and to procure new ones. The opposition leaders were rather unscrupulous in this struggle, publicly accusing each other of mischief, corruption, and even treason and resorting to armed attacks on each others' caravans on Afghan territory. The article "Mujahidin' Outcry," written by an IUMA-3 member, reads:

> There are many IUMA-3 Mujahidin in Afghanistan, and refugees in Pakistan, . . . but unfortunately certain Arab countries have channeled a large part of their assistance to another applicant, that is, to IUMA-7. It is not that we are against help to our Moslem brothers and countrymen, but we do not understand why a particular group of refugees and Mujahidin should get aid that greatly exceeds their needs, while the Mujahidin and refugees belonging to our alliance get no help whatsoever. We get neither clothes, nor food, nor money. . . . Such discrimination is sure to cause a rift in the ranks of the Mujahidin.[29]

A London magazine correspondent in Islamabad, reporting on counterrevolutionary factions and their rivalry and conflicts over the distribution of weapons, wrote that they ". . . carried the counterrevolutionary spirit too far. Some groups at specially arranged press conferences announced that if their rivals got better weapons, they would capture them when they were delivered to Afghanistan.[30] The text of the Afghan Islamic Party (AIP) military commandant's order of 1981 only confirms the report. Paragraph 4 of the order reads:

> The Afghan Islamic Party's Mujahidin brothers must make every effort to discover the whereabouts of other political groups' ammunition stores. If conditions are favorable they must capture them and use the weapons in the interests of the Islamic jihad. In addition to ammunition stores, they may seize weapons and food on the roads.[31]

The commanders of armed opposition units in the field often severely criticized their own parties' leaders in Peshawar, describing certain of them in most derogatory terms. Anwar Amin, a commander of one of the units based in Nuristan, said to a western observer: ". . . they make money out of our blood."[32]

The United States from the very start tried to help the Afghan opposition to overcome its inner conflicts and to unite its forces in the struggle for power. President Ronald Reagan received in Washington on July 16, 1986, a delegation of Afghan resistance leaders headed by B. Rabbani. The delegation included S. Mojaddedi, S. A. Gailani, and M. Nabi Muhammadi. It was not an ordinary delegation. B. Rabbani, the fundamentalist Islamic Society of Afghanistan (ISA) leader, who together with Hikmatiyar put forward the slogan "Neither West nor East," and did not favor any cooperation with the West, led the delegation. Besides himself it included three leaders of traditionalist organizations: the Afghan National Salvation Front (ANSF), the Afghan National Islamic Front (ANIF), and the Afghan Islamic Revolution Movement (AIRM). These leaders had always been rivals despite having a common target, that of overthrowing the Afghan government. It is noteworthy that the AIP leader, G. Hikmatiyar, refused to join the delegation and renounced it. This is another bit of evidence of a split within the IUMA alliance.

Among other things, the delegation at its meeting with President Reagan requested increased American military aid and a supply of sophisticated air-defense weapon systems—the highly effective portable Stinger guided missiles. Reagan approved the request, with the first deliveries of the missiles taking place in March–April 1986.*

Thus, with the help of the United States, Pakistan, and several other countries, the Afghan opposition managed to expand its armed struggle against the government of Afghanistan. Foreign military and financial aid enabled the Mujahidin to combat effectively not just the Afghan regular army but also the Soviet troops who had invaded the country. For nine long years, many thousands of Soviet soldiers were unable to crush the Mujahidin of Afghanistan.

Would the People's Democratic Party of Afghanistan have succeeded in retaining power face to face with the opposition, without Soviet help and without combat operations of the Soviet troops on Afghan territory? The new regime seemed to be backed by the Afghan regular army. This army, which had field experience and rich traditions and was armed with western and Soviet weapons, was initially behind the coup. In order to answer the question, and to understand what caused the Afghan authorities to turn to the Soviet Union for help, and why they were unable to handle the opposition using their own military strength, we should learn a few facts about the Afghan army and its state of readiness in December 1979.

Throughout Afghan history, the army has always played a key role in defending the crown and the government and has supported whatever political policies were being followed both inside and outside the country. The army backed various coups d'état and the coups' success followed those who managed to win the army and, in particular, its command echelon. As a rule, each party developed a wide-scale propaganda campaign to influence the military into supporting its interests. The generals' attitude toward the ongoing reforms in the country was of major importance. Until the late 1950s, the officers' corps in the Afghan army, however, had supported the ruling circles' policies and shared their ideology. But beginning in the early 1960s, Afghan of-

---

*At the time of the request, the American military did not want to allow the Stinger system out of friendly hands. This handheld system continues to be highly effective and could be devastating to commercial and other aircraft if it were to fall into terrorist hands. They also did not want it captured by the Soviets. So this concession to the rebels can be considered of great significance.

ficers, who were stimulated by the progressive political activities of the urban and rural population, plunged into the vortex of the political struggle. Large numbers of noncommissioned officers of technical units (tank, air, engineer, and communications) of the royal army were deployed mainly in the capital and its suburbs. They were particularly affected by the revolutionary spirit, with groups of them developing quite distinct attitudes. Some were supporters of the monarchy, others were adherents of extreme-right clerical circles, and still others were followers of so-called progressive democracy. Finally, a group of radical officers was attracted by socialist ideology that wanted to suppress capitalism in the Soviet manner.

The supporters of the monarchy included mainly generals and other officers who represented the royal court, the tribal aristocracy, landlords with many holdings, and merchants. This group championed monarchist ideas and backed economic reforms and modernization of the state system within a parliamentary monarchy. The king's cousin, Muhammed Daud, was the group's leader and idol. Despite being barred from high political office by the constitution of 1964, he enjoyed influence and authority in the army. Muhammed Daud had won many of his supporters during the period 1953–1963, when the army was used largely at construction sites of industrial enterprises, airports, irrigation systems, and roads. M. Daud drew to himself many energetic officers, and advanced them to key posts in the Afghan army. Some of these officers, who were promoted to high grades, owed their promotions to Mr. Daud's help.

Another monarchist group was also active in the army. It was closely linked to the tribal aristocracy, influential Moslem clergy, and major landowners. The king's uncle, Marshal Shah Wali, was its leader. Commanders of air force and air-defense troops were active members of this group. Characteristic of this group were extreme Pushtun nationalism and a desire to save the monarchy and to strengthen the influence of Islam in all spheres of life. Its members saw efforts to expand economic and political ties to the outside world as highly desirable. They also hoped to procure military aid from both the USSR and the United States. Many officers belonging to the group graduated from American military courses. They favored ties with the United States and were opposed to closer links with the USSR.

The followers of the extreme right were quite numerous among the senior officers of the Afghan army. They had an ultrareactionary approach to home social problems, a drive toward international isolation, and hostile attitudes toward democratic reforms. However, the group was far from being united. Religious conflicts split the group. For example, officers who came from Kabul and its suburbs revered well-known religious leaders from the Mojaddedi family; those who came from Panjsher and Tahav tended to follow the famous Islamic activist Fahr ul-Mahach Ahund-zade Tahavi; those who came from Herat honored the Kyarih clan; from Logar province, Ahad-zade Saib Musa Logari; from Paktia, Seid Moktab Saib.

As we see it, the political climate in the Afghan army was determined by a series of factors. Things could go in opposite directions very easily. Some would want to maintain national unity, whereas others were ready to lead a revolution. The military could support the regime or cause it to be replaced.

At this time, a group of young officers who shared republican ideas and supported large-scale social and economic reforms came to the fore. Most of these officers had graduated from military colleges in the Soviet Union and other Eastern European countries. On September 17, 1964, an illegal Army Revolutionary Organization (ARO) was set up, a direct result of these young officers* being influenced by Communist politics. This new organization adopted a program and a charter that was influenced by both international and domestic situations. It felt the urgency of setting up a revolutionary organization and spelled out its aims and priorities along a general Communist party line. The ARO program stipulated an armed uprising by workers and peasants, civil and military intelligentsia, craftsmen and merchants. The army was supposed to play the key role. Deposing the king and setting up a socialist government that would set the country on an anticapitalist path were seen as the first priorities.

---

*The leaders of this clandestine faction of young officers were Faiz Muhammad, Pacha Gul, and Abdul Hamid. Faiz Muhammad was ambushed and killed by the *Mujahidin* in 1980. Pacha Gul has had a varied career, acting as ambassador in a number of diplomatic posts, but had been working secretly as a *Mujahidin* agent for ten years before defecting to Peshawar in December 1989. He now is an adviser to Gulbuddin Hikmatiyar. Adbul Hamid is a political chameleon, changing names and allegiances whenever convenient. As the PDPA dies he will probably try to switch sides again, but it is unlikely that anyone will trust him.

In spite of the fact that the young officers' program attracted many supporters in the army, they failed to make their organization strong and united enough to reach their goals. To our thinking, one of the reasons for their failure was the fact that there was no competent leader with charisma, which was a very important attribute for the Afghan officers.

Muhammed Daud* succeeded in becoming such a leader within his political group. Being a member of the royal family, he could overcome to a certain extent the functioning of the old regime supporters. The young ARO officers realized this fact and it prompted them to establish contact with Mr. Daud's friends in the early 1970s. The young officers had reason to believe that if they could combine forces, it would help them to overthrow the monarchy.

The preparation of a coup by the left-wing officers and Mr. Daud's supporters was carried out in great secrecy. Still, the first attempt, undertaken in the spring of 1973, failed in its purpose. The antimonarchist organization in the army was exposed, with its members facing a threat of physical extermination. This caused the opposition to speed up its preparation for the coup.

In midsummer 1973, the conditions to carry out the plan were most favorable. Mass discontent with the policies pursued by the monarchist regime was mounting. The king left the country to take medical treatment abroad. This made the struggle for power easier. Moreover, it allowed Mr. Daud to avoid a delicate dilemma in determining the fate of the monarch, his cousin, after he was deposed. Under the pretext of a military exercise, the troops were issued ammunition and fuel for the vehicles, allowing the plotters to move the troops and thus fulfill the plan of the coup without bringing any suspicion upon the army.

We should emphasize that, given the estimated balance of forces in the army on the eve of the coup, the monarchy was still strong enough to defend itself. Its most ardent supporters, among them the king's son-in-law, Gen. Abdul Wali, in particular, sensed the pending revolt in

---

*Muhammed Daud was an experienced politician who, since the 1950s, was a reputed supporter of dramatic reforms in both politics and socio-economics. He was backed by liberal landlords, members of the small middle class, influential theologians, and tribal leaders.

the army and were ready to undertake a preventive purge within the ruling clique. They would create a military opposition, and thereby save the monarchy. However, the antimonarchist forces moved first and forestalled the loyalists and completed their work successfully.

The coup d'état started on the night of July 16, 1973, with the seizure of the royal palace and the arrest of the king's family. All channels of communication were cut that connected the government and the senior military command with the troops and police. High-ranking civil and military officials were arrested. Important government offices, such as the post, telegraph, and telephone offices, the bank, and the airport, were occupied. All the roads leading to the capital were blocked and the Central Corps headquarters and units that might be used to defend the old regime were paralyzed. The commissioned and noncommissioned officers of the 4th and 25th Tank Brigades, the commando battalion, the communication regiment, and some of the units of the royal guard took the most active part in carrying out the coup. Neutral officers joined the supporters of the coup when they felt that the balance was tipped in favor of the new regime. When the news was sent out, remote garrisons added their support for the coup.

Shortly after the coup the supreme ruling body of the country, the Central Committee of the Afghan Republic, was set up. The military activists of the coup were heavily represented in the body.

So the monarchy in Afghanistan was overthrown in July 1973 by the army, with the PDPA playing the crucial role. Having entered the republican central bodies of power, the left-wing officers had the power to influence the new regime's program policies.

Analyzing the existing information, we have come to the conclusion that between the overthrow of the monarchy and April 1978, the political doctrines that formed the basis for the army's ideology did not change. Although the ideological structure remained the same, its components, such as faithfulness to the primary traditional spiritual values of Islam and its binding religious rites, hindered achievement of socialist ideals.

To strengthen its position in the army, the Daud group began a series of incentive measures, mainly concerning activists of the 1973 coup. Certain officers were promoted two grades higher; the length of service in a regular grade was cut; all sergeants were promoted to junior lieutenants; and young officers were appointed to important posts in the central command, staff, and troop units. It is interesting, considering the leftist politics of the regime, that most of these young officers had been in the Soviet Union. By the end of July 1973, all the members of the military forces took an oath of allegiance to the new republic.

The military command was purged, but not extensively. It eliminated only men who were most odious to the new government, such as the Central Corps commander, Maj. Gen. Abdul Wali; the minister of National Defense, General of the Army Khan Muhammed; the Central Staff chief, Col. Gen. Hulini Faruk; and a few others. The majority of conservative generals and senior officers either retained their posts or were given other appointments. In protecting the old army elite, Mr. Daud, no doubt, hoped to broaden the degree of his support in the army. He was fully aware that the army was his main pillar of strength and that if he lost it, his power would be eroded seriously.

As could be expected, the reactionary monarchist faction was very reluctant to lose the army also. In just six weeks after the deposition of the monarchy, a large antirepublican plot was exposed. Behind the plot was the military who previously had strong ties with the royal court, such as the old air force and air-defense commander, retired Colonel General Abdurrazak; the former governor of Nangarhar, retired Lt. Gen. Khan Muhammed; and retired Lt. Gen. Muhammed Rahim, the earlier police and gendarmery commander.

Another plot, no less dangerous to the regime, was also connected with the army. It was staged by a faction of a right-wing political organization affiliated with the Moslem Brotherhood. The plot was forestalled in December 1973; however, this did not prevent certain forces from making new attempts to overthrow the republican regime with the help of their supporters in the army.

New large-scale plots were initiated by certain prominent Moslem leaders in July 1975 and December 1976. The latter was headed by the commander of the artillery department of the national Defense Ministry, Maj. Gen. Said Mir Ahmad Shah. The aim of the plotters was to depose the republican government, eliminate the Communist influence, and establish a theocratic state.

During the years of political struggle in the country, 1973 to 1978, the People's Democratic Party of Afghanistan (PDPA) considerably strengthened its position. By April 1978, the military adjunct of the

PDPA numbered more than 2,000 commissioned and noncommissioned officers in its ranks.[33]

Of utmost importance to the PDPA military units were organizational arrangements aimed at preparing the party's cadres to act under emergency conditions and be able to control other military units. There was a carefully elaborated plan that included participation in exercises and rehearsals, intimating that actions contrary to the government were imminent and being countered.

The developments to come provided a deep insight into the motives of the PDPA leaders, whose tactics were to develop their influence within the army.

During April 1978, the struggle between the two main factions in the political development of Afghanistan reached its peak. On the one hand, the Daud regime was trying to fulfill its pledges and strengthen its power. On the other hand, dissatisfied as they were with the government, its reforms, and the inconsistency of democratic changes, the PDPA leadership demanded Mr. Daud's resignation. These developments took a very rapid turn.

The funeral of one of the PDPA leaders, Mir Akbar Khaibar, who was killed by terrorists on April 17, 1978, took place two days later. The event grew into an impressive march of thousands of people, which degenerated into a political demonstration displaying antigovernment posters and signs.[34] The government characterized the march and the displayed slogans as "illegal and unconstitutional." It was decided to arrest the general secretary of the PDPA Central Committee, Nur Muhammed Taraki, the secretary of the Central Committee, Babrak Karmal, and several other PDPA leaders. Various officers known for their opposition views were also arrested.

The situation that the PDPA leadership had foreseen and that their military cadres had been trained to handle thus emerged.

On the morning of April 26, as soon as the news of the PDPA leaders' arrest was reported, the PDPA Central Committee made a decision to start the revolution by the army. It was scheduled for 9 A.M. the next day. Without any delay, communications were secured with the leading party cadres in the army who served on the air force and air-defense staff. They were deployed in the Khwaja Rawash district in the northeastern suburb of Kabul, not far from the international airport. According to the plan of the uprising, officers who were PDPA members were appointed to command the revolutionary units. The plan of the uprising stipulated:

- announcement by Maj. M. A. Watanjar of the Fourth Tank Army headquarters of the start of the army advance at 9 A.M., April 27;
- seizure by the tank units of the radio station "Radio Afghanistan" and other key posts in the capital, and shelling the presidential palace;
- taking control over the principal army units to prevent their possible use by the Daud government to protect its interests;
- blocking the 7th and 8th Infantry Divisons with the help of anti-aircraft batteries deployed in and around Kabul in case the divisions attempted to support the Daud regime;
- occupying the Khwaja Rawash airport and Bagram military airport (sixty kilometers north of the capital) and making the aircraft ready for combat raids;
- if necessary, launching air attacks against any resisting forces;
- organizing a broadcast by Radio Afghanistan to inform the people of the revolutionary coup of the armed forces.

The events proceeded according to schedule. On the evening of April 26, Kabul radio broadcast the Daud government statement about the arrest of the PDPA leaders. The news stirred a wave of discontent in the army. After the broadcast, the military minister, Gulam Haidar Rasuli, issued an order to bring all army units into combat readiness, and to arrange rallies in support of the Daud regime on the morning of April 27.

This decision was a mistake on the part of the government because it gave a warning to the PDPA members and influenced them to keep in touch with each other and better coordinate their activities for the uprising.

At 6:30 A.M., April 27, the revolutionary officers, who were all PDPA members, gathered near Dehmazang, one of the districts in Kabul. They received their assignments and then traveled to their service posts on buses that regularly took the military to their units.

At 9:00 A.M. Major M. A. Watanjar, addressing his military subordinates at the Puli-Charki garrison, thirty kilometers east of Kabul, announced the start of the uprising. Following the announcement, party supporters prepared the tanks and armored personnel carriers for the march. The commander of the 15th Tank Brigade, Gen. Muhammed Ysuf, tried to stop the rebellious officers but failed. He was confined and all the combat vehicles went into rebel hands. At 9:30 A.M. the telephone line connecting the Defense Ministry with the Puli-Charki garrison was cut off.

At about 11:30 A.M., the first tanks under Watanjar's command left the garrison and headed for the capital. They were soon followed by other armored vehicles from the garrison. All in all, there were 250 tanks and armored personnel carriers available to the rebels.

Very soon, the presidential palace, where the cabinet was having an emergency meeting, was surrounded by the rebels. In response to an ultimatum demanding his resignation, M. Daud ordered the guards still loyal to him to open fire at the rebel forces with artillery and automatic weapons.

At the same time, at the air force headquarters near Khwaja Rawash airport, heavy fighting broke out between old regime supporters and the revolutionaries. Colonel Abdul Qadir, the chief of the military revolutionary committee, flew there immediately by helicopter. With the help of a tank unit that arrived just in time, the airport was occupied, and the entire garrison joined the rebels. Under Abdul Qadir's orders, aircraft took off and headed for Kabul. At about 4 P.M. this air strike force attacked the presidential palace. Tanks and armored personnel carriers attacked the main governmental offices in the capital and occupied the prison, and the PDPA leaders detained by the Daud regime were set free. At 7:00 P.M., Radio Afghanistan reported the victory of the April revolution.

Not everything took place smoothly, of course. Heavy fighting broke out in the northwestern, southwestern, and western suburbs of the capital. In particular, the 7th and 8th Infantry Divisions' garrisons, along with the 88th Artillery Brigade and the Central Corps headquarters, experienced severe combat. By dawn on April 28, however, the joint efforts of the rebel tank and air units overcame the resistance in these garrisons. The presidential palace fell. Killed in the shooting were President Daud; his brother, Muhammed Naim, Minister of State for Foreign Affairs; Vice President Abdullah; and the interior minister.

The army units deployed in the provinces did not actually take part in the uprising. But this did not stop them from joining the revolutionary forces after the occupation of the presidential palace had been reported. Soon, the Kandahar, Jalalabad, Herat, and Ghazni garrisons and the military airports of Shindand, Mazar-i-Sharif, and Kandahar were under the control of the rebel officers.

Representatives of the armed forces were appointed as members of the newly formed Revolutionary Council. At its first meeting on April 30, 1978, they elected Nur Muhammed Taraki as their chairman and the head of government (prime minister). Babrak Karmal became the deputy chairman of the Revolutionary Council. The supreme body of state power proclaimed the country the Democratic Republic of Afghanistan (DRA) on April 30.

A day later, the DRA government was formed. It included twenty ministers and their deputies. Three military activists of the April events received appointments in the cabinet. Col. Abdul Qadir was appointed minister of defense, Maj. M. A. Watanjar the deputy prime minister and minister of communication, and Maj. Muhammed Rafii the minister of social work.

The new Afghan government put forward a program of wide-scale reforms, including land reform, elimination of feudal relations in the rural areas, industrialization of the country, guaranteed rights and freedoms, and equal rights for women. It was planned to purge counter-revolutionary elements from governmental bodies. Measures to strengthen the Afghan army and to allow the military to take an active part in the country's social-political life were worked out.

As for foreign policy, the DRA intended to pursue an independent peaceful policy of nonalignment, of a positive and active neutrality. It called for good and neighborly relations with all countries in the region, and especially for strengthening and developing even more friendly relations with the Soviet Union.

The reform program and measures to purge "hostile elements" from governmental bodies and the army caused protests by many political and religious leaders, high-ranking personnel of the army, and some tribal leaders. Driven out of the country into neighboring states by the revolution, they began to set up bases for training armed units. Rather strong military groups were even being formed illegally in Afghanistan itself. The governments of neighboring Iran and Pakistan assumed an openly hostile attitude toward the new Afghan government.

Under these circumstances, the DRA needed a powerful army, able to withstand the opposition and defend the regime. A series of steps designed to strengthen the armed forces were taken.

In the spring and summer of 1980, border troops, which included *tzarandoy* ("people's militia") units, were formed.

To stabilize the personnel of the armed forces and to try to ensure their loyalty, the government issued a decree under which the enlisted military, the heads of the Pushtun tribes who had done great service to the country, and the peasant families whose sons volunteered for enlistment in the army were given preferential treatment in their land allotment.

To further strengthen the armed forces, the Supreme Military Council on January 9, 1981, adopted a law requiring universal military service. Under the law all young men who reached the age of nineteen were eligible for immediate army service. Voluntary service in the National Afghan Army was still encouraged and continued to play its role.

The Supreme Defense Council, replacing the Supreme Military Council, was set up in August 1981. Allotted state and military power, the council was charged with mobilizing the population to rebuff outside aggression and the internal counterrevolution. Responsibility for the overall organization of the armed forces also rested with it. The Supreme Defense Council included both military and civil leaders. Babrak Karmal, who at that time was the PDPA general secretary, headed the new council.

Military and political training were added to the curricula of schools and colleges, and boarding schools were opened for children whose parents were killed in the ongoing civil war.

A Chief Political Department was set up in the Afghan army; its main mission was to educate soldiers, most of whom came from peasant families, in party doctrine. Gradually, PDPA sections (party committees) were created in each battalion, regiment, and division. Commissioned and noncommissioned officers and private soldiers were encouraged to join the ranks of the PDPA. To us, this is quite reminiscent of what we have been used to in the Soviet Army.

In 1982 the Central Committee of the PDPA and the DRA Revolutionary Council decided to initiate an effective complex military-political system "to defend the revolution and the people." The army, border troops, tzarandoy, state security bodies, units of the revolution defenders, and tribal volunteer units were all to become integral parts of the system.

As a result of these and other decisions, the Afghan armed forces grew to 130,000 people from about 100,000. Commanders were chosen chiefly from officers who had been trained in the Soviet Union. They were all either PDPA members or its supporters. The army was equipped with Soviet tanks, armored personnel carriers, aircraft, and small arms.

One might suppose that this rapid reorganization of the army and the new supplies of sophisticated weapons would provide a reliable defense for the regime. Still, the DRA authorities appealed to the Soviet Union for more military aid. Why?

It has already been mentioned that the Afghan army included many tribesmen who kept close ties with their friends even while performing service to the state. It is only natural that animosities for the regime felt by this or that tribal group would influence their representatives in the army. In addition, practically every tribe had its own armed bands in various stages of combat readiness. They were able to defend their own interests and were capable of many years of struggle. These were the same factors that eventually drove the country from monarchy to a republican regime and then to the April revolution of 1978.

The PDPA, which came to power with its own socialist philosophy and ideas, split the country into two opposite camps. Party actions that followed, such as unjustified use of force, mass arrests, and executions without trial, alienated a considerable number of the working people, including tribesmen. This was exacerbated by too rapid land reform and other reforms as well as an ongoing power struggle within the PDPA leadership. Economic difficulties, which included shortages of necessities, also aggravated the political situation.

Mass emigration followed. The most numerous Pushtun population moved from Afghanistan to the border area of Pakistan. Most tribal chiefs and Moslem leaders moved from general opposition to the DRA government to an active struggle against it.

Beginning in 1980, more than four hundred armed units of about forty men each were active in combating the government in guerrilla actions. Six thousand people were active in Nangarhar province, three thousand in Zabul, and three thousand more in Helmand. The units were recruited mainly from the local population (85 percent), with the rest from those who had previously emigrated to Pakistan and Iran. Normally, units were formed by decisions of tribal or clan elders' jirgas.

It was the *jirgas* that appointed the commander, choosing him from the leadership of rebel organizations located in the region. Moslem leaders or mullahs frequently headed such units. For example, in 1981 in Paktia, provincial armed units were formed under the command of the local leaders of the Afghan Islamic Party (AIP, Hikmatiyar), the Islamic Revolution Movement of Afghanistan (IRMA, M. Nabi Muhammadi), and the National Front of Islamic Revolution of Afghanistan (NFIRA, S. A. Gailani).

A large percentage of units (more than a quarter of all Mujahidin formations) acted under the leadership of the AIP. They were deployed in all border provinces as well as in Laghman and Logar.

As a result of combat operations, as early as 1982 the units controlled more than 90 percent of the territory of Paktia province. In Laghman province, government forces lost control of 75 percent of the inhabited area. A similar situation prevailed in Logar province, where the opposition controlled 85 percent of the villages.

Discontent with the PDPA policies continued to grow in the country and it had to affect the army, lowering its combat readiness. It became clear to the PDPA even by the end of 1979 that the party could no longer control the situation in the country without outside support.

We estimate that there were at least 40,000 Mujahidin operating in Afghanistan at the start of 1980, with more joining their ranks daily.

There were more than 400 antigovernment armed units in the Pushtun tribes region alone, making up some 20,000 people. The command elements of these units were located primarily in Pakistan. Situated in Pakistan were not only commanders of the armed units but specialists in mine laying and advanced weapons. Troops from the Afghan mountains area were being trained at special bases in Pakistan (Aravali, Mirkhani, Baghi, Badabar, and Miramshah).

The Mujahidin struggle was continuing to gain momentum using the powerful pull for the people of the Islamic jihad. It gave their combat activities a religious connotation and basis that became very important for the movement, since it brought the Mujahidin an aura of Allah's warriors engaged in a just struggle to save the motherland and fulfill the will of the Most High.

Meantime, the situation in the country for the government and the army was worsening. Increasing numbers of alarming reports from Afghanistan, coming to the General Staff of the USSR armed forces between March and November 1979 through the Soviet chief military advisor and military attaché in Afghanistan, caused considerable concern in Moscow:

> The entire country has been swept by armed uprisings. There are armed revolts in the army.
>
> March 15–20: An upheaval in Herat, with local garrison units taking an active part in it. The revolt was suppressed by the troops loyal to the government. Two Soviet military advisers were killed in the fighting.
>
> March 21: A subversive plot in the Jalalabad garrison was exposed. About 230 plotters, all of them military, were arrested.
>
> May 9: mass antigovernment armed uprisings occurred in Paktia, Ghazni, Nangarhar, Kunar, Balkh, and Kabul provinces. All these actions were suppressed by troops loyal to the government.
>
> July 20: An uprising in Paktia province was suppressed. The rebels attempted to occupy Gardez, the center of the province. Two Soviet advisers were killed in the fighting.
>
> August 5: Mutiny in the 26th Airborne Regiment "Commandos" Battalion, deployed in Kabul. As a result of bold steps, the mutiny was suppressed. The Kabul garrison has been alerted for action, condition 1.
>
> August 11: In Paktia province (Zurmat region), as a result of heavy fighting with superior forces of the rebels, the 12th Infantry Division suffered large losses. Some of the governmental soldiers surrendered; others deserted.
>
> The struggle between President Taraki and Foreign Minister Amin is intensifying. The two party factions, Parcham [banner] on one side and Kalq ("people") on the other, are in opposition to each other. Mass arrests and executions of rebels are under way.
>
> September 14: At 9:30 A.M. units of the Kabul garrison were placed on alert. Chief of the General Staff Yaqub ordered the troops to occupy their operational positions in the city. At 5:30 P.M. Kabul radio broadcast a decision to release M. Taraki from all his posts. The presidential residence is under the control of the troops, with all communications cut off. Commanders of the 8th Infantry Division, artillery regiments, and a special tank battalion, as well as chief of staff of the 4th and 15th Tank Brigades, have been removed

from their posts and arrested; air flights have been banned. What is happening is a military coup.

October 10: M. Taraki is reported to have died on October 9 "after a short but fatal disease." Our information is that Taraki was killed by guard officers at 11:30 P.M., October 8, under Amin's orders.

October 16: From 11 A.M. to 3:10 P.M., Kabul garrison units were engaged in heavy fighting with insurgent units of the 7th Infantry Division. The revolt was suppressed with the help of aviation and tanks. The mutineers had risen to remove Amin from power. The officers who initiated the revolt disappeared. Chief of the General Staff Yaqub exercised command over the forces that suppressed the mutiny. The situation in the country and in the army remains extremely complicated.

The Soviet leadership's concern increased dramatically toward the developments in Afghanistan. What was happening could hardly have been unexpected, with the possible exception of Taraki's assassination. For more than a year, the country was being battered by domestic conflicts and unrest in the army. The PDPA leadership kept up a constant number of appeals to the Soviet Union for help. It is interesting to look at the list of requests made by the Afghan government in 1979. All of these concerned bringing various contingents of Soviet troops into Afghanistan. The classified messages were passed to Moscow from Kabul:

April 14: Send to Afghanistan fifteen to twenty Soviet helicopters with crews.
June 16: Send Soviet tank and armored vehicle crews to guard the government and Bagram and Shindand airports.
July 11: Bring some Soviet special groups, up to a battalion each, to Kabul.
July 19: Bring into Afghanistan up to two divisions.
July 20: Bring into Kabul an airborne division.
July 21: Send to Afghanistan eight to ten Mi-24 helicopters with Soviet crews.
July 24: Bring to Kabul three military units.
August 12: A priority deployment of Soviet Army units into Kabul

is urgent. Send to Kabul three Soviet special forces units and transport helicopters with Soviet crews.

August 21: Send to Kabul 1,500 Soviet paratroopers. Replace Afghan antiaircraft crews with Soviet troops.

August 25: Bring more Soviet troops into Kabul.

November 17: Bring a special battalion to secure Amin's personal safety.

December 2: Forward a reinforced regiment to Badakhshan province.

December 4: Bring Soviet militia units to the northern area of Afghanistan.

December 12: Deploy Soviet garrisons to northern Afghanistan; establish defenses on Afghan roads.

The following reports were transmitted to Moscow by A. Puzanov, the Soviet ambassador to Kabul; B. Ivanov, a KGB official (State Security Committee); L. Gorelov, the chief military adviser in Afghanistan; I. Pavlovsky, general of the army, commander in chief of the ground forces, and deputy defense minister of the USSR; and Col. Gen. S. Magometov, the chief military adviser in Afghanistan since November 1979.

. . . was invited to visit comrade Amin. At the request of M. Taraki he was asked to send to Kabul fifteen to twenty helicopters with ammunition and Soviet crews to be used in case of emergency in border and central regions against mutinous troops and terrorists infiltrated from Pakistan. Comrade Amin assured me that the arrival of Soviet crews in Kabul and their participation in combat would be kept secret.[35]

Both Taraki and Amin more than once returned to the issue of expanding the Soviet military presence in the country. They want about two divisions to be brought into Afghanistan in case of emergency "at the request of the legitimate Afghan government." Concerning the request by the Afghan leadership, we replied that the Soviet Union could not do it. . . .[36]

At our talks on August 10 and 11 with H. Amin, he said it would be possible to use the troops deployed in Kabul against the mutineers when the Soviet leadership responded positively to the request made by the DRA government and M. Taraki himself. This concerned the deployment in the Afghan capital of three Soviet special forces battalions. At the request of H. Amin on August 12, the chairman of the state security service, Sarwari, asked us to speed up the fulfillment of the request put forward by the DRA leadership concerning the deployment of Soviet special battalions in Kabul and transport helicopters with Soviet crews.[37]

On August 11, there was a meeting with H. Amin at his request. Much attention was given to the question of bringing Soviet military units into Afghanistan. Amin earnestly requested that the Soviet leadership be informed about the urgency of bringing Soviet units to Kabul as soon as possible. He said more than once that "the arrival of Soviet troops would boost our morale and imbue us with confidence and peace of mind." He went on to say, "The Soviet leadership must be concerned that its opponents in the world may see this as an interference in Afghan internal affairs. I would like to assure you that we are a sovereign independent state and thus will settle our problems independently. . . . Your troops will not take part in combat actions. They will be used only at critical moments. I think there will be a need for Soviet units until spring."[38]

. . . was invited to see Amin on August 20. At the talks Comrade Amin said that large quantities of troops, including those with heavy weapons (tank, artillery, and other units), concentrated in the Kabul region could be used against revolutionary forces in other areas if the Soviet Union agreed to send 1500 to 2000 "commandos" (paratroopers). They could be deployed in the Bala-Hissar fortress. . . . Then, Comrade Amin raised a question of changing the crews of the seventy-seven Zenap antiaircraft batteries deployed on prominent heights around Kabul for Soviet ones, since he doubted the loyalty of the Afghan crews.[39]

. . . had a meeting with H. Amin on December 3. During the talks H. Amin said, "We intend to transfer a part of the personnel and weaponry of the 18th and 20th Divisions (from Mazar-i-Sharif and Baghlan) to form people's militia units. In this case instead of bringing Soviet regular troops into Afghanistan, it would be better to send Soviet militia units, which together with our militia units could provide security and restore order in the northern Afghan regions."[40]

*   *   *

These reports show that in asking the Soviet Union to bring troops to Afghanistan, the Afghan leaders had in mind different kinds of troop contingents: helicopter crews, antiaircraft gun crews, security units to guard the government, paratroopers, and even Soviet militia units.

These same Soviet officials in Kabul sent to the Kremlin a number of reports, urging the Soviet government to bring into Afghanistan a few Soviet units "under a decent pretext." They were concerned over security during a possible evacuation of Soviet citizens from Kabul if the situation became more aggravated. Their requests were partially satisfied.

In particular, on July 7, 1979, an airborne battalion under Lt. Col. A. Lomakin's command was secretly brought to the airport in Bagram under the guise of their being technical specialists. They came under the command of the Soviet chief military advisor and did not interfere in the affairs of the Afghan government.

After H. Amin came to power, the Soviet leadership sent through its officials a series of recommendations for measures to stabilize the situation. It also reaffirmed its support, while at the same time denouncing the campaign of repression against the supporters of the former president.

A special Soviet Foreign Ministry ruling, signed by A. Gromyko, the Soviet foreign minister, was passed to Kabul.

To Soviet officials in Kabul:

1. Taking into consideration the real state of events in Afghanistan, it is believed expedient that Soviet officials should not refuse to deal with Amin and his team. It is necessary to do everything possible to keep Amin from repressions against Taraki's supporters and other people who fell into his disfavor who are not enemies of the revolution. Contacts with Amin should be used to learn more of his political outlook and intentions.

2. It is also thought expedient that our military advisors to the Afghan troops as well as advisors in the state security service and the Interior Ministry should stay where presently located. They should fulfil their direct functions, connected with plans and the conduct of combat actions against rebellious units and

other counterrevolutionary forces. It goes without saying that
they should not take any part in repression against those who
fell into Amin's disfavor, if the units that they are advising
are used for this purpose.[41]

Meanwhile, the developments took an inconceivably rapid and
unpredictable turn when Soviet planes landed paratroopers in Kabul.
The first action, carried out on December 27 by Soviet special units
together with Afghan units of opponents of Amin, was the storming
of Amin's residence in Darulaman. Amin was killed in the fighting,
and his regime was overthrown.

At the beginning of the fight, Babrak Karmal, guarded by his supporters, arrived at the Chihulsutan guest residence of the Afghan
Council of Ministers, where he received the news of Amin's death.
After that, Karmal addressed the people of Afghanistan over Kabul
radio.

Soviet units then took control of the key regions in the country. Together
with the Afghan army, they safeguarded administrative centers, vital
installations, airports, and main highways.

Thus began a new page in Afghan history, tragic for Afghanistan,
tragic for the Soviet Union.

NOTES

1. *Newsweek* "Afghanistan, a Spring Offensive." (April 20, 1981).
2. *Times* "Afghan Resistance: Divided, the Rebels Fight On." London (February 9, 1982, p.8).
3. N. Joshi, "Intervention in Afghanistan," Foreign Affairs Report, N. D., Vol. XXIX, No. 7, 133.
4. J. B. Ritch, Hidden War: The Struggle for Afghanistan, staff report prepared for the Committee on Foreign Relations, U.S. Senate, April 1984, 14.
5. *Figaro* "Le Levier Afghan" (July 3, 1979, p. 346).
6. J. Stork, U.S. Involvement in Afghanistan, MERIP (Middle-East Research and Information Project) Reports, N.Y., 1980, No. 89, 25.
7. F. Ahmed, interview, MERIP Reports, N.Y., 1980, No. 89, 1.
8. A. Arnold, *Afghanistan: The Soviet Invasion in Perspective* (Hoover Institution, Stanford [CA] 1981) p. 104.
9. J. Stork, U.S. Involvement in Afghanistan, 25–26.
10. B. G. *Asnad-e lanah-e jasusi*, No. 30. "Afghanistan-2," Teheran, 114.
11. Ritch, "Hidden War," 27.
12. B. G. *Asnad-e lanah-e jasusi*, No. 30. "Afghanistan-2," Teheran, 31.
13. *Newsweek* (May 28, 1979).
14. Reported by TASS in the USSR, January 22, 1980.
15. Ritch, "Hidden War," 14.
16. B. S. Gupta, *The Afghan Syndrome: How to Live with Soviet Power.* (Delhi: 1982), 42.
17. A. S. Waliullah Khan, "U.S. Backed Emigre Afghan Government in Pakistan." *Blitz*, India (January 9, 1980.): 20.
18. *Ash-Shaab* (January 25, 1980).
19. M. S. Kazim, "Advocates of Extremism." *Al-Kifah al-Arabi*. No. 18 (1979).

20. "A Question of Firepower," *Far Eastern Economic Review*, Vol. 114, No. 53, Hong Kong (1981): 25–26.
21. *International Herald Tribune* (September 11, 1984).
22. *Middle East International*, No. 147, London (April 5, 1985): 11.
23. *International Herald Tribune* (November 29, 1984).
24. *Attehad-e-Mujahidin* (November 19, 1984).
25. *Al-Sobh*, No. 2 (April 1980).
26. "Victory Is in Bravery," *Kiyam-e-Hak,* No. 5, Peshawar (1985): 5–6.
27. *Asnad-e lanah-e jasusi, Papers of a Spy Nest*, N 29, Afghanistan, Teheran, n.d. Foreword.
28. T. Amin, "Afghan Resistance: Past, Present and Future," *Asian Survey*, Vol. 24, No. 4, 379, 397 (1979):
29. *Attehad-e-Mujahidin* (November 19, 1984).
30. *Middle East International*, No. 247, London (April 5, 1985): 11.
31. *Attehad-e-Mujahidin* (August 15, 1982).
32. *Middle East International*, No. 247, London (April 5, 1985): 14.
33. *New Age* (September 23, 1979): 13.
34. *Haqiqat-i-Inqilab-i Saur.* Kabul (April 4, 1980).
35. L. Gorelov, April 14, 1979.
36. B. Ponomaryov, July 19, 1979.
37. A. Puzanov, B. Ivanov, and L. Gorelov, August 12, 1979.
38. L. Gorelov, August 12, 1979.
39. I. Pavlovsky, August 21, 1979.
40. S. Magometov, December 4, 1979.
41. A. Gromyko, July 15, 1979.

Soviet army tanker trucks transport fuel to the Kabul garrison.

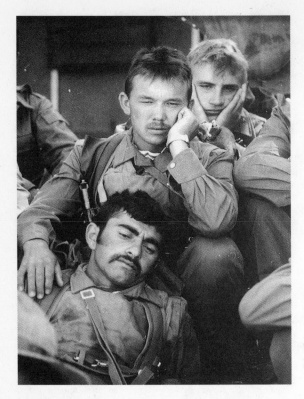

Tired soldiers returning to Russia as the war ends in 1990.

Soviet motorized troops returning to their homeland.

Soviet tank commanders salute their commander as they return from the Afghan war.

A long convoy crossing into the Soviet Union in 1990.

Evidence of the destructive force of a land mine.

A lonely Soviet soldier mans a typical observation post in the Afghan mountains.

General of the Army Valentin Varennikov, former USSR First Deputy Defense Minister, army commander-in-chief and chief military advisor in Afghanistan. One of the 1991 coup plotters, he is now in prison.

Col. Gen. Boris Gromov, commander of the Fortieth Army, whose troops performed the bulk of combat operations.

A major Afghan leader, Jaqub Khan, chief of the Baluch people.

Soviet artillery concludes a fire mission in support of ground troops.

Soviet medium caliber artillery bombarding a *Mujahidin* position.

Soviet gun-howitzers in the midst of a fire mission.

Soviet tanks in a tactical training exercise.

Little victims of the Afghan war.

This young man smiles despite the loss of his arm.

Soviet and Afghan casualties.

Afghan village destroyed by artillery fire.

Villagers try to live among the ruins of their village.

A *loya jirga* in session. The *Mujahidin* leaders are debating their next blow against the government.

Mujahidin warriors captured by Soviet troops.

A Soviet army military police checkpoint. The truck driver's documents are being examined.

Soviet army soldiers check a road for land mines. Dogs were used to good effect for this kind of mission.

These Soviet soldiers gingerly remove a land mine from a road.

Mujahidin leaders plan an operation.

Mujahidin guards at a training center in Pakistan.

Mujahidin soldiers at a rally.

Mujahidin gunners aim a handheld Stinger antiaircraft missile launcher. This surface-to-air missile (SAM) came from the U.S. inventory.

Gulam Rasul, commander of a large *Mujahidin* field detachment.

Soviet air force pilot Col. Alexander Rutskoi. He is a veteran of the Afghan war and is vice president of Russia at this writing.

Colonel Ruslan Aushev, Hero of the Soviet Union. He commanded a motorized infantry regiment with distinction in Afghanistan. Later, he was a member of the USSR's Supreme Soviet.

Colonel Aushev relaxing with some friends.

Poor horse; poor soldiers.

A Soviet general decorates one of his soldiers.

Afghan government troops on parade in Kabul.

Afghan troops in dress uniforms.

Afghan troops on parade in field uniforms.

Former prisoner of war (POW) Nikolai Ryzhkov at a press conference on July 27, 1991, at the Novosti Press Agency.

Former POW Oleg Khlan at the same meeting sponsored by the Public Committee for Liberation of Afghan POWs.

The father of POW Kur-
banali Tashrifov comes to
Pakistan to take his son
home after seven years in
captivity.

After six years as a POW Sergey Tseluzhevsky is reunited with his parents.

Former chief of the Signals Department of the Afghan Ministry of Defense, Abdul Wodood. He was executed for his complicity in the murder of President Taraki.

Said Ahmad Gailani (center), acting president of the *Mujahidin* provisional government, presenting Soviet POWs Andrey Lopuh and Valery Prokopchuk to the USSR's ambassador to Pakistan, V. P. Yakunin (left).

Babrak Karmal, former leader of the PDPA and Revolutionary Council of Afghanistan.

Soviet attack helicopters operating in Afghanistan.

Soviet pilots scramble for a mission.

Afghan army soldiers man an antiaircraft mount.

A Soviet army patrol struggles over rough terrain in Afghanistan.

Chapter 3

IN THE COMBAT AREA

────────────────
▬▬▬▬

FIRST LESSONS

Soviet troops deployed in Afghanistan encountered quite unusual situations and missions. Nothing of what they had to deal with under those conditions had anything in common with what they had seen at training centers or maneuvers. Nothing of the kind could be found in field manuals and in the training programs of Soviet military academies and colleges, where Soviet commanders had studied the art of war. In Afghanistan they had to learn again, to gain experience and knowledge that could be of real use in offense and defense, in crossing ravines and canyons, coordinating assaults, both ground and air, and guarding against ambushes while on the march. Such experience was accumulated literally day by day in small doses, taking a long time.

Initially, Soviet troops in Afghanistan were made up of the following formations: three motor rifle divisions, an airborne division, two supply and support brigades, and several separate regiments, which reported to army headquarters. These formations were under the command and control of the Fortieth Army. Later, it was named a Limited Contingent of Soviet Troops in Afghanistan, a strange-sounding military appellation.

As the Fortieth Army was formed in the Turkestan and Central Asian

Military Districts, the number of Central Asian and Kazakh nationals of Moslem origin was significant among the personnel of the troop units. The Soviet government considered this a positive factor, since it made linguistic contact with the Afghan population easier. And, indeed, the majority of Soviet soldiers could communicate with the locals, which initially facilitated accomplishing their combat objectives. But later this played a negative role, because in many cases these relations assumed the character of fraternization between Soviet soldiers and the Mujahidin. A regular commerce between them, including trade involving narcotics, proved to be a real problem to commanders. In a number of cases, to make matters worse, Soviet soldiers who were Moslems deserted their units and went over to armed groups of the Afghan opposition and fought against their old comrades. It soon became evident that the national composition of the Fortieth Army had to be changed. Later in the war, it was staffed mainly by Russian soldiers.

Moral and psychological indoctrination of the soldiers, where they learned the peculiarities of life in Afghanistan and their roles in combat operations, proved to be most important. This inevitably led to changing the entire system of recruit training. But it should be stressed that from the very first, many complications and problems became obvious. On the one hand, there was no theoretical doctrine that might be helpful in the moral and psychological training of soldiers. Before the soldiers could be truly effective in combat against the Mujahidin, these problems had to be solved by intensive training. On the other hand, hiding the truth about the war in Afghanistan influenced the psychological condition of soldiers negatively and contributed to low morale. Although it was detrimental for them to be far from home and be experiencing the fear of death or being wounded, the realization was that back home their families did not know the truth about the war and could not understand the situation as it was in Afghanistan. All this influenced the emotions of the men. It became a very hard war. There is no wonder that it was called "the Soviet Vietnam."

Certain irregularities were found in the system of preparing young soldiers for army service. They saw the war as it entered their lives through many hardships, far from the motherland, in an unusual situation, with their comrades-in-arms being constantly killed in combat. The High Command had the difficult task of helping each soldier to adapt to the situation as quickly as possible, to get ready for combat under extreme conditions.

The low level of training of recruits was evident in their inability to react to the demands of military service. Many of these young people were not motivated to serve the country and were used to idleness. They had few experiences in good interpersonal relations and suffered from a lack of responsibility. We estimate that at least 90 percent of the young men who arrived at the training centers of the Turkestan Military District did not have the slightest idea of any of the difficulties of military service in Afghanistan. The training course had to be prolonged from one to six months under the guidance of officers with combat experience who acted as the instructors. Special training exercises for soldiers and officers lasting twelve days were particularly important. In organizing this course, the primary emphasis was placed on perfecting combat training.

The training was divided into two major parts. At first, everything necessary to strengthen the motivation of soldiers and their understanding of the importance of the tasks facing them was accomplished. The instructors sought to ensure that the soldiers were confident in the use of arms and other combat equipment, and thus be capable of fighting the Mujahidin effectively. To accomplish this, both the capabilities and limitations of the enemy were emphasized. The second stage was to train the soldiers in their individual and collective combat skills. Unit combat actions and psychological readiness for fighting in specific types of combat were the goals of training in this second stage. Close attention was paid to specific soldiers' skills, such as helicopter crews, drivers, scouts, engineers, artillery observers, and signal specialists.

Commanders were enjoined to support the morale of these young soldiers to improve their attitude and make them confident in working with their comrades. To achieve this aim, special groups were formed consisting of three soldiers and a sergeant with different lengths of service. The idea was to help the recruits adapt to combat conditions. A specific problem that received emphasis was the difficulty that soldiers had who had to remain at remote posts for long periods of time. The following fact testifies to the importance of this situation. While in Afghanistan, a division was usually assigned up to 500 outposts along a line several hundred kilometers long. A regiment had more than a hundred of these outposts in a line approximately 130 kilometers long. The loneliness and boredom experienced in these remote outposts were extremely detrimental to the morale of the soldiers who manned them.

Because of the secrecy surrounding the war in Afghanistan, great efforts were made to indoctrinate the soldiers politically. This veil of secrecy extended, of course, to the Soviet mass media and was also of great importance.

Commanders had special problems in the training of junior officers. To a great extent they were due to the low level of professional military qualifications of the officers sent to Afghanistan. They had a general lack of experience and skills that might have enabled them to lead their men under the hard conditions of Afghanistan. Recent graduates of military academies and those officers who had served in units with reduced numbers of soldiers were especially disadvantaged. So, after initial setbacks, it was decided not to send any young officers to Afghanistan immediately after graduation. They were required to serve at least a year in an appropriate unit. But, this was no solution for the problems.

Many officers tried to adopt a kind of indifferent method of dealing with soldiers. Their custom was to wait for a senior's command and use no initiative, to see themselves as only executing a command. It took months after officers arrived in their units in Afghanistan to correct deficiencies in the practical skills of working with people under combat conditions. The soldiers' low level of military and professional competence was a continuing problem for the high command. The situation was exacerbated in some cases by mistakes of personnel staffs who knowingly sent to Afghanistan those officers who either had bad overall records in service or had serious flaws in their relations with soldiers under their command. Added to this situation was that many commanders, especially in the first years of the war, conducted operations based on their experience in maneuvers oriented to western regions. Much of the training was conducted on such a basis. At various conferences, they discussed at length how harmful anything new in concept was, so that the search for new or unconventional means of fighting this type of war went no farther than studying the experience of the last time we had been at war.

Finally, they saw that they had to abandon the entire system of training officers. They then organized it in stages, including four days' training in the military district and a week-long assembly of different categories. They covered the history, geography, and other peculiarities of Afghanistan, of the enemy's tactics and those of Soviet troops in the mountains and desert. They trained with all types of arms and combat equipment, but in more realistic situations.

As a result, things improved. Soviet soldiers were beginning to learn to fight, to get used to new tactics better suited to this strange war.

At the same time reorganization of motorized infantry units took place. These units were equipped with more modern weapons and lighter equipment. Training of commanders, staff officers, and units fighting in the mountains became more focused. Initially, this new training was conducted at camps in the USSR. Two motorized divisions were trained under the new guidelines in the Turkestan Military District. Training for units in-country went on concurrently in Afghanistan. To improve coordination within the units, during intervals between field operations, training grounds were built in garrisons, fire bases, and depots, to include special tank roads.

Special training of units for specific operations against the enemy proved extremely useful. Such training as a rule occurred a day or two before the raid or other military operation.

Perfecting officers' skills in fire control during combat operations was also very difficult. We have alluded several times to the general poor state of training of the young officers sent to Afghanistan. Although conditions improved somewhat over time, this situation continued throughout the entire war. Soviet units suffered failure on many occasions because personnel lacked training in specific skills.

The overall composition of the Fortieth Army was getting better, in that units that were ill-suited for operations in the Afghan mountains were withdrawn. They were mainly tank regiments, as well as heavy artillery and mortars and towed air-defense weapons. What was needed were light, highly mobile forces that would not have the same difficulties as the heavily equipped formations under the conditions of Afghanistan. It became absolutely obvious that it was necessary to send the heavy units back home. Highly mobile weapons systems proved effective, such as infantry fighting vehicles, amphibious trucks, and light reconnaissance vehicles.

Most of the units entering Afghanistan in 1979–1980 had well-trained personnel and modern equipment. Infantry and artillery soldiers and other specialists knew their organic weapons systems well. When mounted in vehicles they understood, they fought in units with great coordination and were well orientated. But, as it soon became clear, this was true only while operating on flat terrain.

Massive employment of armored vehicles was hindered by the mountainous nature of much of the country, where steep slopes as well as narrow ravines limited their movement, preventing tanks and infantry fighting vehicles from being fully deployed. Other problems for the mechanized forces were the soft sand in the desert and swampy terrain in some areas.

In fighting with the Mujahidin, tactical air landings were widely used for securing dominating heights and blocking areas where the enemy troops were located. Again, these kinds of operations had to be conducted by light infantry forces.

Normal functioning of the troops was dictated by local conditions. Since there are no railroads in Afghanistan, everything necessary for sustaining the troops and their combat operations was delivered by truck convoys, with only a small part carried by air. There were only two land routes: Termez–Kabul and Kushka–Kandahar. It was vitally necessary to protect these roads in order to avoid losses of equipment and personnel in the vehicles. The Mujahidin naturally knew this and concentrated their ambushes on the roads, to deprive Soviet units of supplies and capture the goods for themselves.

Of all the Soviet troops in Afghanistan, some 35 percent were protecting communication lines and outposts. Prior to Afghanistan, with our European mentality who had ever designed training courses or devised plans to accomplish this kind of mission? Battalions and regiments had to be detached for this duty. For months at a time, soldiers had to stay on dominant features, on heights far away from one another, surrounded by the enemy. We can only imagine the personal problems they had individually and with each other. Squads of seven to twelve had to live in shelters constructed largely of the materials at hand. They had their combat equipment and weapons, and very little else.

Food, water, ammunition, firewood, and coal, as well as everything else they needed, were delivered to them by truck or air every two, three, or four weeks. As with all soldiers, morale suffered when mail from home and loved ones arrived only after long delays. Detached from the situation today, we wonder what they could have talked about and how they could have lived like that for long days, weeks, months, and years. But they did manage to survive and serve and accomplish the combat missions assigned them.

Other units fulfilled quite different tasks from time to time. One battalion would be assigned as an escort for a transportation column; another would be protecting the route. Commanders had to be flexible in determining priorities for the activities of their troops. It was necessary to search for nontraditional forms and methods of managing people of different levels of training and combat experience. Each time something new was introduced, problems increased.

The Soviet command concentrated on helping soldiers overcome the Afghans' hostility, strengthening the Afghans' trust in the troops. It tried to establish close contact with all levels of Afghan society, but this was not easy. The situation was made more difficult by the general state of underdevelopment in the populace as well as the great variety of ethnic structures. Soviet soldiers did not understand tribal psychology, with the strong influence of family leaders, religious authorities, and Islam as a religion.

The Soviet command tried to ingratiate themselves with mullahs, tribal leaders, and local authorities. This was somewhat successful; many of them agreed to friendly overtures to avoid bloodshed and loss of life. This work, added to measures aimed at achieving higher levels of professionalism in troop units, brought some results, causing a reduction of personnel losses.

Mountains and high desert characterize 85 percent of Afghan territory. Unfortunately, in many units the experience and equipment necessary for operations in such terrain were lacking, particularly when the troops were first deployed. These deficiencies caused mission failures and unjustified losses of men, supplies, and equipment.

For example, in the summer of 1980 in the vicinity of the city of Asmar, a Soviet motor rifle battalion was advancing along a ravine deep in the mountains. There, an Afghan government battalion had been blocked by the Mujahidin and was fighting them. But the Soviet battalion coming to their rescue could not move very quickly. The column first ran into an ambush, and then a mined sector of the road. The fight was lost and both units suffered considerable losses.

This and similar defeats in Afghanistan made the Soviet command arrive at some practical conclusions. They began to pay attention to march discipline and coordination among the different services. They started to emphasize mine clearing and night operations. The problem of command and control was addressed, as well as providing the units with necessary supplies consistent with their combat missions.

The drawbacks encountered in the first period of the war included:

- a lack of sufficient practical skills in dealing with personnel in training and the unavailability of ammunition, training aids, and other supplies.
- officers' failure to demonstrate decisiveness and initiative in accomplishing combat tasks when fighting, waiting for prompting and the advice of seniors. They tried to act by rote without taking into consideration the nature of the terrain and the situation at hand. They displayed indecisiveness in maneuvering their forces.
- difficulties in organizing and conducting reconnaissance missions as well as ambushes by the enemy in the mountains particularly, and the desert. Units were poor in target acquisition.
- lack of experience in organizing and conducting combat activities in the dark, especially in the mountains.
- poor knowledge of their basic combat equipment. They were not sufficiently familiar with the T-62 and T-55 tanks with which they were equipped. Previous primary training had been on the newest types of tanks, such as the T-72 and T-80. Their skills were lacking in the use of equipment to prepare for firing.
- poor understanding of the evacuation of combat vehicles from the battlefield under enemy fire as well as the organization and functioning of maintenance assets under field conditions.
- lack of experience in coordination, command, and control of units and fire support in mountain combat and enemy-held territory.

GUERRILLA WARFARE

The enemy developed their tactics and combat techniques to be suited to the terrain and conditions in their country. They did this under the guidance and ideals of Islamic ideologues by planning and waging a guerrilla type of war against both government troops and the Soviet invaders.

The combat actions of armed formations were based on the following main principles:

- avoid direct combat with regular forces when they are numerically stronger, thus avoiding complete destruction of the rebel formations.
- avoid combat actions that would result in position warfare; give up terrain as necessary to preserve the fighting force.
- emphasize surprise offensive actions as a primary precept of fighting, particularly at night.
- use terror and ideological influence over Afghan army personnel and the local citizens.

The success of the Mujahidin in combat had to be dependent on the joint actions of groups and detachments having different tribal and political orientations. But despite differences among the tribes and leadership, the armed opposition represented a well-trained enemy. Its personnel were true to Islam, which demanded that each member of the faithful had to consider the war as his personal affair. Discipline and responsibility were enforced with the threat of harsh measures, including the death penalty in extreme cases.

The fundamental tactical principle of guerrilla warfare was to avoid open actions with large Soviet regular forces and to act in small groups that surprised their foes.

A good example of this was the Panjsher operation in April 1984. The leadership of the Mujahidin avoided defensive combat with Soviet and Afghan forces, instead withdrawing its main forces from danger and sheltering them in mountainous regions. They kept only small detachments available for reconnaissance and ambush. Soviet troops eventually had to withdraw, and the Mujahidin were able to return safely from the mountains and reoccupy the territory temporarily abandoned. In certain provinces, their aim was to capture major administrative centers and occupy certain critical terrain. Such actions, as a rule, were planned and executed in provinces close to borders where it was possible to ensure quick reinforcement and, in case of reversals, to retreat easily across the border. Defensive combat activity was resorted to only in the case of an unexpected assault when there was no path of retreat.

In the holy war against the government, the Mujahidin leadership took a page from the Red Chinese book by not only involving their detachments and groups already available, but also the major part of the population. They were thus able to conduct ambushes (particularly against units on roads) and attacks on posts, garrisons, and the civil government.

To avoid losses from aviation and artillery fire, the rebel detachments stayed dispersed, often, as with the Vietnamese rebels, living among the local populace, periodically changing their locations. Being armed with light weapons and knowing the terrain well, the armed groups maneuvered constantly, showing up unexpectedly in different regions. They usually stayed in one place no longer than twenty-four hours.

In all cases, surprise was utilized in operations, coupled with great initiative in maneuvering their forces and independence of operations. The rebel detachments were able to fulfill their plans as a result of good intelligence and being warned of Soviet operations against them. When they mounted an operation, they performed it rapidly. They quickly disengaged and withdrew under cover along routes chosen beforehand.

Following their tactics, the insurgents attacked Soviet troops while they were advancing to contact, in the objective area, and most often when they were returning to their bases. Usually, small columns were attacked; those with poor security on the march and without air protection suffered badly. To perform more serious tasks, such as attacking and occupying military garrisons and major administrative centers, the rebels brought together coordinated formations of as many as 2,000 men. If they failed in such a major attack, they retreated to Pakistan for replenishments in personnel and weapons. But usually, they abandoned the concept of a real front line, and infiltrated through the positions of Soviet troops at night to reach their objectives. They then occupied advantageous positions and began to fire on the unsuspecting Soviet troops at dawn. The rebels were masters at sniper fire.

Psychological warfare was an important adjunct to the rebels' armed attacks. They used disinformation, spreading false rumors about the location of troop units and the whereabouts of their leaders. Quite often they used Afghan and Soviet military uniforms in their deception campaigns.

The combat skills of the Mujahidin were constantly becoming better. They acted more cautiously, avoiding risks as they perfected their guerrilla warfare. They paid special attention to the best tactics of ambushes and raids.

Ambushes were carefully planned and organized by groups of from fifteen to a hundred men. Ordinarily, the ambushes were set up on roads in order to destroy military columns as well as convoys carrying civilian cargo. When choosing the place for an ambush, the rebels were careful to exploit the features of the terrain. They looked for ravines, narrow places, and mountain passes. The positions were developed beforehand in great secrecy, picking convoys' rest stops, where the troops' security would be minimal. The rebels were always careful, before organizing an ambush, to conduct a careful reconnaissance of the enemy and the terrain where it would take place.

The rebels sent out as reporters small groups of three or four men, usually unarmed and disguised as local citizens. They then deployed a fire group to destroy personnel and equipment and a blocking force of four or five men to prevent the enemy's possible retreat from the ambush zone. They kept a reserve unit that occupied convenient fire positions to reinforce the fire or blocking forces, and as a covering force if retreat were necessary.

When attacked the rebels tried to cover all their enemy's main forces. They were careful to designate routes of retreat and assembly points. Usual weapons of the group included two machine guns, a mortar, three grenade launchers, several sniper rifles, and assault guns, such as captured AK-47s.

Participants in a typical ambush took positions along a road at a distance of about two hundred meters, separated from one another by about thirty meters. When the Soviet column entered the killing zone, the rebels directed fire first at vehicle drivers and command personnel. Then they began to fire at trucks carrying personnel. Simultaneously, grenade launchers were fired at armored vehicles escorting the convoy.

Raids were frequently resorted to by the rebels. Their plans involved secret approaches to the objective, security during the raid, and quick retreat after the mission was completed. Before a raid, they carefully rehearsed their assault plan, using terrain similar to the real thing. Various guard posts, small garrisons, depots, and bases were chosen for raids.

Careful reconnaissance was considered necessary, and their advance march was kept secret. Front and flank scouts were assigned who were positioned on dominating terrain features. A point patrol of two or three men who were disguised as peasants or shepherds was placed within sight of the command and control personnel.

The raiding force was usually composed of about thirty men, divided into smaller groups that included fire and maneuver elements and engineer support. The main attack force of the raid destroyed the objective. In withdrawing, the raiders broke into smaller groups and left the area along different routes.

In addition to the above-mentioned types of action, the rebels conducted harassing fire at outposts and other targets. They infiltrated their cadres among the local population in villages, especially in the "green zone," where they conducted economic sabotage.

The rebels usually began a raid or other such operation about an hour before dark and completed it rapidly, especially if they were not successful. If that happened, they quickly disengaged and retreated under the cover of night along routes they had chosen beforehand.

They created bases in Afghan territory to support and sustain their operational forces, adding them to those already under their control. The Afghan bases were situated mainly in the mountains, and whenever possible near the headwaters of rivers. Bases such as these proved to be extremely advantageous in supporting their tactical concepts. A valley situated at the headwaters of a river usually begins in high mountains. The Mujahidin used this feature to keep from being blocked or surprised while in camp; it denied the Soviets a convenient approach. Sometimes, air landings were also impossible because the terrain was so inhospitable.

At the entrance of such a valley, armed groups of rebels created a system of deeply echeloned ambush points and obstacles by using natural and artificial shelters in the rocky soil. They integrated these obstacles with a well-organized firing plan using both direct and indirect fire. Deep in the valley, they maintained supply dumps of weapons, ammunition, and other material. Caves were used for personnel and headquarters shelters.

At all dominant features of the terrain, positions were developed for air-defense machine guns, which were sited to fire at both air and ground targets. Alternative locations were developed for these and other positions. Included were camps, bases, communications, and maneuver routes.

These defense positions established by the Mujahidin at the entrances of ravines were extremely powerful, with logical approaches mined. Often mines with additional amounts of explosives of up to fifteen kilograms were employed one under the other, with a dirt layer between them. Roads were prepared for destruction in the event of Soviet penetration. Observation posts were situated at a distance of up to a hundred meters from one another in such a way as to allow visual communications between them. Radios were also used when available.

Double or triple defense lines were established with the aim of destroying offensive enemy forces in echelon. The first line of defense of six to eight men, having delivered their fire on the enemy, retreated quickly to the second line, joining the second group of defenders. After that, both groups retreated to the third line. If they had done their work well, there was no need for them to relocate any farther. Very often this was the case.

In the length of a valley or ravine there would be maneuver groups positioned who could assault the advancing enemy from the flanks and rear. They tried to exploit gaps in positions of Soviet and Afghan troops, infiltrating under cover of darkness. At dawn they would begin to fire at troops who were ill-prepared for such treatment.

Rebel units in such an ambush were split into several groups with different missions. One would act as observers; another was to capture prisoners, supplies, equipment, and weapons; the third was organized to intercept and destroy reinforcements before they entered the combat zone.

When the ambush began, snipers would fire at drivers and commanders' vehicles, hoping to slow up the movement of the convoy. They fired simultaneously at the head, center, and tail of the column. Armored cars were engaged by heavy machine guns whose fire was aimed at the tires. Personnel carriers were destroyed by the fire of grenade launchers. After that, the rebels covered their relocation through the use of mortar fire, both preplanned and adjusted.

Sometimes the insurgents used special operations such as ruses and feints, which distracted the enemy's attention and confused his command element. Rebel soldiers were placed in the main zone of the ambush.

This group would fire unexpectedly at the Soviet column. The idea was to get the enemy troops to advance quickly to hit a relatively weak adversary. The column was thus subject to the fires of the main force of the rebels, causing heavy losses.

The rebels especially liked to attack single vehicles and small columns where overwhelming firepower could be employed. The rebels, like the Vietcong, did not ever want to engage the Soviets in "set piece" battles. They would inflict an unexpected blow and then withdraw quickly, as their enemy evacuated the dead and wounded.

When organizing ambushes in built-up areas, armed groups were concealed behind walls and in buildings. They tried hard to remain undetected, letting Soviet reconnaissance and security forces go untouched. When the Soviet main body approached, the rebels began to fire from loopholes, windows, and doors, concentrating mainly on fuel and ammunition trucks. When the assault began, coordinated fire would be directed from small arms, machine guns, and grenade launchers. Later, more intensive fire at selected targets was conducted, most effectively from both sides of a road. This proved to be the most dangerous for Soviet columns.

The heaviest possible casualties occurred when all of a column was allowed to enter the ambush site before well-aimed fire began. By destroying vehicles at the beginning and end of the column, they created jams. Frequently, destruction would be complete as their enemy milled around in panic.

The rebels moved armed formations from one region to another with the aim of deceiving the Soviet High Command on their overall strength and disposition in an area. Because of these successful deception operations, Soviet planners had a difficult time directing air or land assaults against them. Groups and detachments were forbidden to remain for more than one night in each place. Nights were used for marches and movements to planned areas of operations. Routes of advance were chosen far from main roads, which helped the rebels conceal themselves while moving. Several hours before the march, a reconnaissance patrol was sent in advance. If regular troops were detected on the chosen route, it was immediately changed to an alternate one.

In 1987–1989 the rebels began to pay much more attention to the fight against helicopters and other aircraft. They studied the vulnerable points of Soviet planes and the direction of their flights. They organized an observation network. Especially effective was the use of the portable American air-defense Stinger missile systems, which inflicted heavy losses on Soviet pilots.

In analyzing the combat potential of the Stinger missile, the Soviet High Command came to the conclusion that front and army aviation could successfully overcome them if they resorted to active and passive jamming and countermissile maneuvers. The use of such defensive methods by helicopter pilots greatly lessened the intensity of infrared radiation of the engines. This caused retargeting a missile to be much more difficult for the soldier firing from the surface. Nevertheless, the combat effectiveness of Soviet air operations was lessened greatly when the Stinger was introduced into Afghanistan.

By the mid 1980s, other improved armaments were provided to the rebels. A squad of ten men had one machine gun and nine automatic rifles. A platoon of twenty-five was equipped with a recoilless rifle, a machine gun, and sixteen assorted small arms.

Despite overall heavy losses suffered by the Mujahidin from combat actions by Soviet troops, their organization and strength in Afghanistan did not change particularly, remaining quite stable. This was achieved by constant replenishment of the units due to the arrival of trained troops from Pakistan added to recruiting and conscription in Afghanistan. We estimate that every month, up to eighty groups numbering about 2,000 men were sent to Afghanistan. Numerically stronger groups were concentrated in the central, northeastern, eastern, and southeastern zones, where there were up to a thousand detachments of 43,000 men—about 70 percent of the total number of Mujahidin. Air-defense systems were concentrated in regions along the Pakistan border, where large numbers of rebel troops, bases, camps, and other installations were located. In addition to the Stingers, the air-defense systems used cannon of 14.5mm and heavy-caliber 12.7mm machine guns. The rebel soldiers regularly used small-arms fire for air defense.

SOVIET OPERATIONS

Depending on local conditions, geographical features in the various areas of Afghanistan were taken into consideration when plans were made to commit Soviet troops to combat. The northeastern and eastern parts of the country are mountainous and 3,000 to 5,000 meters above sea level. Actions involving tanks and artillery were highly restricted there, and helicopters could fulfill tasks only at service ceilings.

The western part of the country is less mountainous, allowing wider use of tanks, infantry fighting vehicles, and artillery. There were fewer restrictions on the use of helicopters. In the south, there are extensive desert regions that allow massive use of all services.

Throughout the country, particularly in the mouths of rivers, green zones and villages were encountered. In inhabited areas, Soviet and Afghan troops frequently conducted joint operations.

Combat actions were planned to provide for the use of separate battalions and even companies. Transportation of such units into combat areas to attack objectives was often accomplished by helicopters, which immediately after landing began fire support missions for the troops they had transported.

A significant peculiarity of combat actions in mountains is that the usual three- to five-times superiority needed by the attacking force in a conflict to defeat the defenders does not necessarily hold true. In this situation, the ability to use fire and maneuver in light of the terrain at hand and the camouflage capability of both sides are determining factors in who gains the victory. Effective command and control during hostilities is probably more important in this kind of warfare than in a typical fight in, say, the steppes of Russia.

As we have said, Soviet troops in Afghanistan used air landings and airlift of combined arms units very widely. The composition of landing forces was variable, from company size to a division. The sizes of landing zones in mountains are different from those of the "classic scheme." In high mountains, the size of the zone can be significantly less than in usual moderate terrain, fully corresponding to the demands of specific combat situations.

Air landings on October 25, 1984, are an example of what we mean. On a single day 1,280 men were airlifted from the Bagram airfield to the vicinity of the Pizgoran ravine. This was accomplished by twenty-four MI-8 helicopters. Only one helicopter was lost after the landing. The helicopters were used as shuttle airplanes to deliver the troops by small loads. They were protected by MI-24 helicopters and MIG-23 and SU-25 high-performance aircraft.

This deployment tactic allowed the troops to inflict losses on those in defensive positions, with concentrated fire at distant operational locations beyond the front line. They were able to successfully destroy fortified objectives and to defend an airhead once established. Later, main force units effected a linkup with the airborne troops. Together they conducted a decisive attack and advanced further into the enemy's defensive positions.

The tactical use of this air-landed force allowed a successful river crossing that in turn permitted a high-speed offensive attack against the enemy. But, at the same time, the full potential of such airborne tactics was not realized, because soldiers of motor rifle units were poorly trained in firing from helicopters in flight. Furthermore, commanders had only a vague notion of the maximum combat and transport capabilities of helicopters as well as specific means of organizing and coordinating their operations. In other words, they succeeded in this operation despite their ineptitude, probably because they surprised their foe.

The success of combat actions of airborne units to a great extent is determined by the quality and secrecy of training. This includes developing the plan of combat operations, informing all personnel of the plan, and providing the units with whatever they need for the combat to come.

The experience of paratroopers in preparing to operate in Kandahar in mountainous terrain can be used as an example. They were able to complete the entire mission while the region of operations and its nature were kept secret. In the units, soldiers received special training in different disciplines, such as marksmanship, reconnaissance, engineering, map study, and medical aid. They also trained hard in coordinating with artillery and aviation units under conditions similar to actual combat. The training was completed with platoon live-fire exercises. Some companies, which by the plan were to act separately, took part in company tactical maneuvers with live fire and coordination with supporting artillery and aviation assets. Beyond that, they prepared their combat vehicles, weapons, and other combat material for the operation and provided all personnel with the special supplies and equipment they required.

The advance of the troops to the designated area of operations was organized in a combined manner—from their dispersed camps, by transport aircraft to assembly areas in the vicinity of the mountains and from these by helicopter to the landing zones. Combat vehicles and artillery went separately at night. It took ten to fourteen MI-8 helicopters to airlift one reinforced airborne company to the highlands, because at an altitude of 2,000 meters, one helicopter can carry only six to eight paratroopers; at an altitude of 4,000 meters, only four to five men. Each helicopter was assigned an alternate landing zone in the event that the initial and even secondary landing had to be aborted.

To prevent rebel raids and the seizure of vital areas and villages by them, government army troops set up blocking positions on a line-by-line basis. They set up position after position across the slopes of mountains, concentrating closer columns of reconnaissance troops on the high ground and security troops wherever needed.

Special attention was paid to detecting mined obstacles in places suitable for ambushes. But it was difficult to detect mines and booby traps in rocky soil, so the movement of units was inhibited. The speed of movement in mountain terrain was only one kilometer an hour without enemy interference. When they encountered any enemy resistance or when the terrain was unusually rugged, their movement was even slower.

Helicopter gunships were used widely, along with 122mm howitzers and self-propelled artillery. Antitank guns and guided missiles had no ordinary targets but were useful in destroying pinpoint hardened targets sheltered by rocks and in caves. Observers in the units were trained to control and adjust the fire of aviation assets of all kinds as well as artillery and mortars.

Divisions were usually dispersed by regiments, battalions, and companies to cover an area of 250 square kilometers. Each regiment, battalion, or company stationed in a separate garrison was assigned a sector of terrain, within the limits of which the commander was to conduct reconnaissance missions as well as operations against rebels in coordination with the Afghan army.

But dispersing the troops in such large territories created difficulties in unit control and made ordinary tasks more complicated. Located as they were in separate garrisons, independent actions undoubtedly caused platoon, company, and battalion commanders great problems. Adding to their difficulty is the fact that officers of the Soviet Army were not normally encouraged to display much individual initiative. In the Afghan situation, independent actions became a necessity, frequently with bad results. But in time the officers began to adjust.

Success can be described in the combat actions undertaken in the Paktika-Urgun region in February 1983. Seven reinforced Soviet battalions and 19 battalions of the Afghan army equipped with 38 tanks, 218 infantry fighting vehicles, and armored personnel carriers made up the attacking force. Artillery support for troops consisted of 157 guns, howitzers, and mortars.

By the time the operation began, reconnaissance assets had detected concentrations and active well-organized defenses of some 32 groups of Mujahidin in the area of Urgun. These units comprised about 3,500 men, equipped with 7 tanks, 9 guns, some 15 mortars, more than 40 machine guns, air-defense systems suitable to the mountains, and many small arms.

By occupying dominant terrain features along the Urgun ravine one by one, army airborne units facilitated the advance of armored cavalry units and then heavy equipment. Afghan units blocked the dispersed detachments and groups of rebel soldiers. In their operations, both Soviet and Afghan troops called for tactical aviation and artillery support as needed. But whenever possible, the troops' movements were performed at night without fire support and battlefield illumination, allowing them to hit the enemy unexpectedly in their flanks and rear. Using these tactics they were able to block the rebels' retreat and destroy them in detail.

Similar operations were conducted from December 1983 to November 1984 in the regions of Herat, Kabul, Kapisa, Farah, and Parwan. Individual actions lasted from six to eighteen days. The density of tanks used to block the movements of the rebels was from six to ten vehicles for a single kilometer of the front, whereas for infantry fighting vehicles and armored personnel carriers, about thirteen to eighteen tanks per kilometer were used. This provided for reliable fire support of the dismounted units.

As we mentioned earlier, the terrain varied in different parts of the country, making it difficult for Soviet troops to adapt. They had trouble exploiting the terrain tactically when they were in other than mountainous areas. In forested regions as well as oases and other green zones, Soviet troops suffered heavy losses and had little success. They learned, first of all, that they could not use armored vehicles effectively there. Commanders initially were unskilled in planning for such combat situations and coordinating troop movements and fire control. Armored units in this type of terrain as a rule did not enter green zones, but instead were used for passive blocking missions, which deprived the assaulting units of their main advantage over the enemy. The problems of using vehicles in Afghan forests and green zones should have been anticipated, because the situation is the same as in ordinary forested areas anywhere in the world.

A good example of such problems is the May 1984 operation at the Fahdja oasis. For the second time Soviet paratroopers tried to enter an armed rebel base in a lush green area. As long as the armored cavalry was able to support the paratroopers with fire, they managed to enter the green zone and to advance with some difficulty up to a depth of some three hundred meters. After that advance, the attack failed because the infantry was isolated without fire support. Dense and well-aimed fire from strongly developed and well-camouflaged rebel positions pinned down the Soviet soldiers and inflicted serious casualties.

It was getting dark quickly. The battalion commander, Lt. Col. Vladimir Romanov, ordered the units to consolidate at the line they had managed to reach. It was necessary for him to analyze the reasons for the failure without emotion, determine an effective course of action, make a good decision, and get the troops ready to reengage the enemy.

It became evident that the primary efforts of the enemy were directed at depriving the paratroopers of support from their supporting heavy weapons systems and thus change the balance of power to the rebels' benefit. They laid many mines on the roads and flooded fields. They used grenade launcher fire from minimum distances to prevent tanks and other armored vehicles from entering the green zone.

Artillery also proved useless to Soviet troops. Using clever infantry tactics, they initiated fire from an ambush from a distance of only fifty meters, so that rebel troops immediately positioned themselves in close contact with Soviet soldiers. This made artillery fire impossible because of the danger to friendly forces. Artillery observers could not adapt to this cunning, quick, and bold enemy. Only direct fire, when a static target could be accurately identified, allowed Soviet troops to achieve success under these conditions. No less problematic was the use of tactical aviation and helicopter gunships on positions that were practically invisible from the sky. American troops had similar problems in Vietnam.

Romanov's paratroopers on their own found themselves engaged with equal numbers of rebel troops who were more mobile, knew their own terrain intimately, and were able to inflict casualties from positions developed in advance. The parallel to the Vietnam War was evident. This action was a disappointing failure.

But the Soviets had more success in terrain suited to their tactics and equipment. They were able to block regions occupied by the enemy by moving motor rifle units in and on infantry fighting vehicles at night along secure routes to designated assembly areas. They then blocked all usable routes by using mines, obstacles, and fire. They encircled the enemy, dividing the unit into company sectors. At dawn they would land troops by air at distant points, where approaches were difficult.

As a rule, tactical air landings were accomplished by multiple units. For example, in large-unit actions in the Charicar valley in February 1986, on the first day three paratrooper battalions were landed with attached reconnaissance units and three motor rifle companies to consolidate the airhead. In divisional and regimental zones, a density of one motor rifle or paratrooper company with six to ten armored vehicles occupied one kilometer of the line. Later, seventeen more battalions were landed. All in all there were twenty-one battalions and three separate companies, including seven battalions of the Afghan armed forces. To provide for secrecy in this type of operation, motor rifle units began encircling the enemy dismounted.

When it was necessary to isolate the enemy in mountains so steep that armored vehicles could not be used, commanders had to depend solely on air-landed troops. If there was sufficient helicopter support, simultaneous landings from four directions were attempted. Under adverse weather conditions in the mountains, dismounted infantry troops had to march on foot to find, fix, and engage the enemy. This was not, of course, the preferred way.

The troops acted in different and creative ways to mop up the valleys and ravines occupied by the enemy. When there were enough forces, a second mopping up was carried out while others were occupying the high ground. Great importance was placed on occupying the heights. When there were limited forces, different techniques were used. The plan was to occupy terrain on both sides of a ravine or valley. First of all, heights near the entrance to a ravine were seized by motor rifle companies. Later, while the mopping up force advanced along the ravine, other companies were taking the next group of hills. Then, the companies that seized the first high places leapfrogged to the third set, and so on. Eventually, the entire sector was occupied by Soviet troops. In all Soviet maneuvers, it was considered important to continue sufficient pressure against the enemy, including simultaneous attacks, when troop strength permitted, to try to defeat large numbers of the rebels.

While an offensive was in progress in a ravine or valley, operations were usually conducted for several days in a consecutive manner in a single primary direction along the formation's axis. If the enemy's base was in the middle of the ravine, assaults were mounted from both ends of the ravine. When it was possible to approach and encircle the enemy's base, the pressure came from three or four directions. This was easier in mountainous terrain but proved much more difficult in green zones. Here the enemy was able to maneuver freely, often changing his location. Soviet troops had to change the direction of attack often, advancing first in one direction and then in another. Artillery and air support were used whenever possible, seeking to destroy the enemy by fire alone.

As might be expected, airborne troops were better suited for air landing than were motorized infantry. In the latter case, their commanders frequently made errors in phasing the helicopters in delivery of both troops and supplies. They were not as knowledgeable as they should have been in the behavior of the aircraft at different altitudes and temperatures. There were frequent discrepancies in the timing of air assaults against the rebels, some caused by commanders not paying enough attention to enemy troop dispositions, the strength of their fortifications, and the arms available to them. They frequently conducted inadequate reconnaissance of the enemy before beginning the offensive.

It is obvious that combat never occurs without losses. But good commanders try to keep losses at a minimum. Soviet commanders tried to accomplish this from the very first encounters with the Mujahidin. They learned that direct assaults resulted in high casualties, often with unsuccessful missions. So they began to resort to deceptive actions and surprise. This deprived the enemy of the initiative, affecting them psychologically. But it was hard to keep operations secret. The Soviets tried to limit the number of people who needed to know the plan. Sometimes there were information leaks, usually from Afghan sources.

When this happened, the troops encountered organized resistance by rebels already aware of Soviet intentions. Naturally, disaster followed.

But when a commander's foresight in planning deceptive actions was sound, an operation could conclude successfully. This is illustrated by one of the most significant operations in the war in Afghanistan, Operation Magistral, in November–December 1988. Planning for the operation and its execution was uncommonly detailed.

First of all, the terrain up to and within the objective area was studied carefully. Concurrent with this the Soviets learned as much as possible about the defensive dispositions of the enemy, including his capabilities for both direct and indirect fire. Special attention was paid to the Satekundav passage, where the enemy was expected to make a major attack on the Soviet and Afghan troops. The Soviets compared this operation to similar campaigns in the Caucasus and the Carpathians against the Germans during World War II. The commander, Lt. Gen. Boris Gromov, placed great emphasis on keeping the plans for the operation completely secret, to make the surprise complete. To carry out Magistral he had both Soviet and Afghan troops in his task organization. Leaks of information could not be excluded, because many of the Afghan units were infiltrated by the rebels.

Gromov found it difficult to obtain much intelligence on the enemy's defensive system and their crew-served weapons. It is hard to distinguish artificially built enemy defensive positions from natural terrain features. Having studied the combat area and compared the capabilities of his troops to those of the rebels, he decided to resort to deception. He would send paratroops to the passage, hoping that the enemy would disclose his defense system.

Paratroops were airlifted successfully to Satekundav passage and were immediately subjected to fire of antiaircraft machine guns and artillery. This gave Gromov all the information he needed. He quickly ordered heavy air strikes and artillery fire against the Mujahidin positions. In a matter of hours, the major weapons systems of the enemy were destroyed.

The paratroops, commanded by Guard Senior Lt. S. Tkachev and Yu. Gagarin, fought very well indeed. The Mujahidin attacked them strongly by fire from rocket systems and mortars for more than forty minutes. Coordinated with this fire, rebel soldiers in black uniforms attacked the Soviet soldiers from two directions. The paratroops defended in turn with organic machine-gun fire, causing the enemy to retreat. Soon a second attack began, this time from three directions. Again, precise fire by machine-gun crews made the enemy retreat. In one hour and ten minutes, a third attack began, which proved to be the most powerful. Changing positions, the paratroops called artillery fire on themselves, so close was the enemy. In all, six attacks were repulsed that day.

Such success can be attributed to effective coordination of motor rifle troops, with armor and artillery organized to correspond with prevailing local conditions. Correct offensive battle formations allowed each soldier and officer to feel his own proper place in the operation and engage the enemy without excessive control from higher head-quarters. Command and control systems were established to place fire from a variety of weapons systems as soon as enemy forces were detected. We thus managed to impose our initiative on the Mujahidin and force them to accept the place, time, and type of combat chosen by us. Because of an immediate and devastating response, the rebels' own offensive plans and actions were interrupted. When Soviet forces were properly coordinated with fire from all supporting elements, our operations were successful. Unfortunately, this happened only part of the time.

Organizing and conducting operations aimed at destroying the bases of the Mujahidin were extremely complicated. Problems occurred because of the peculiarities of the geography as well as the skilled tactics of the enemy. Throughout the war, reconnaissance proved to be one of the major deficiencies. As we have mentioned earlier, the terrain varied greatly. In some places, access was easy for wheeled and tracked vehicles; in other places only light infantry could operate. An operation might start in the green zone and end in the mountains. The only factor that remained the same was the elusive enemy.

The rebels rejected the idea of fixed defensive positions, preferring instead slow-up tactics and ambushes, with small groups basing themselves in positions chosen and developed beforehand, such as caves, ravines, and narrow passages. They did not defend staunchly their depots and bases; instead, these were sited mainly in border areas in the moun-tains where accessibility was easily denied to Soviet forces. We were forced to fight a war of attrition, with the advantage usually going to the enemy.

It was especially difficult to obtain information on any of the rebels' positions, so weapons systems could not be used to maximum effect before hostilities commenced. Usually, only the most general information about the enemy was available, including their numbers, composition, armaments, and location.

Difficulties were also present in the organization of and coordination between Soviet and Afghan troops. The Soviet high command tried to resolve these differences by placing Soviet advisors in units of the Afghan army that were to be involved in joint operations. Actions to improve coordination that were agreed upon jointly were routes of advance, lines of departure in the attack troop echelons, direction of axes, boundary lines between units, signal frequencies and other communication details, and, of course, liaison with supporting artillery and aviation units.

Successful joint actions in Afghanistan were characterized by preparation of the battlefield by the following:

- delivering powerful artillery concentrations and air strikes against enemy concentrations, his bases, and depots at the beginning of the operation.
- making multiple and consecutive landings by airborne troops to capture dominant terrain features and, if possible, enemy bases. These troops blocked and attacked enemy formations in coordination with other Soviet and Afghan units.
- using many mined obstacles (by both Soviet and Afghan units) to deny routes to the enemy and limit his ability to maneuver.
- exploiting dominant terrain features and using observation helicopters to provide intelligence used for artillery and aviation fire direction.
- using armor in a limited way.
- using nighttime operations to gain surprise and to encircle enemy forces without detection.

Tactical air landings are extremely difficult to plan in joint operations, particularly while maintaining coordination with aviation and artillery support units. Incomplete planning led to disappointing results, frequently because schedules could not be maintained. An airborne unit, for example, might be landed and not be able to obtain the necessary fire support from artillery and tactical aviation units.

In practice, commanding officers of Afghan units were informed about the concept of a planned operation just before it was to start, usually no more than one day in advance and sometimes while the troops were being deployed, two to four hours before troop movement. This was because of security considerations. Soviet commanders rightly thought that Afghan units were infiltrated with Mujahidin spies, so that security would be lost if the Afghans learned of plans too early. Naturally, coordination suffered. We understand that American forces in Vietnam had the same problem when joint operations with units of the army of Vietnam were attempted.

Sometimes the movement schedules to combat zones were announced to assigned troops, then changed, again for security reasons. Planners tried to make these changes in such a way so as not to influence the actual time of the start of operations. But this procedure caused confusion at troop level, with false starts and general reduction of combat effectiveness.

Surprise in such operations was achieved when combat actions were initiated promptly and movements were made quickly from one operational area to another, particularly when aviation was employed to move the troops.

When planning communication coordination, prospective combat zones were studied carefully and the means were assigned that could ensure the fullest command and control. Units that were to fight in mountainous areas were reinforced in advance. When choosing sites for command posts, dominant terrain features near planned assault locations were preferred. This ensured reliable radio communications.

Afghan troops were used to mop up the area blocked by Soviet troops who prevented the enemy from breaking out of the encirclement. Soviet troops also supported Afghan troops with fire whenever possible.

This manner of waging warfare had its weak points too. Movements of armored cavalry groups were often detected by the enemy, allowing them to monitor their activities closely. As a result, the enemy often was able to leave the area before the airborne landings would complete the encirclement. It was frustrating for Soviet troops to attack an area with no enemy present.

Taking this into consideration, Soviet troops began to resort to different tactics in blocking areas where the rebels were concentrated. For example, in good terrain, motor rifle units mounted with infantry fighting vehicles and armored personnel carriers after a night march were deployed into the encirclement from four directions simultaneously. When this tactic worked, the encirclement was quickly narrowed and the enemy did not have enough time to break out of the area before the final assault.

In different and more varied terrain, the motor rifle units making the encirclement left their assembly areas dismounted and secretly occupied positions on heights close to the area where the enemy was concentrated. Armored cavalry and tank units moved from their assembly areas later and at dawn closed the encirclement from the best direction available. Then, at the same time, Afghan troops began their assault and mopping up.

But we must restate that very often the Mujahidin managed to withdraw their detachments from dangerous regions before being assaulted. In some cases they used secret paths to withdraw. To combat this, Soviet planners tried to use ambushes at probable routes of retreat and, with sufficient forces, double encirclements.

There were times when commanders tried to move the troops too rapidly in the mountains. Actual operational experience showed that the real speed of an offensive in mountain terrain was no more than one kilometer per hour. In the mountains troops had to dismount. The armored troops confined themselves to ravines and valleys and tried to support the dismounted infantry with fire. In effect, in offensive operations in mountains, the armored groups were used as separate elements in battalion combat formations. This applied also to combat formations of regiments and divisions. Reconnaissance was performed by committed units both before the actions were to begin and during their combat exposure. As in all operations, for the entire duration of the war, the Mujahidin enemy were hard to locate and engage. Real intelligence was difficult to obtain, just as the Americans found in Vietnam. There were many parallels between the two wars. From our viewpoint, it is unfortunate that our leaders did not draw the proper inferences from their own experiences with their Vietnamese allies over many years. As in Vietnam there was no strict border between front and rear. Similarly, there was no chance for close contact with the enemy unless they wanted it. They also could not be identified readily because they wore common civilian clothing.

To obtain useful information from reconnaissance, the High Command had to organize ad hoc means. Each battalion in action was assigned a reconnaissance platoon, although such a unit was not included in the formal Table of Organization for the battalion. Also, sufficient troops to man two to four observation posts were assigned to units attempting to perform ambushes. Sometimes, even though their mission was only for information gathering, reconnaissance units actually engaged the enemy and defeated his units.

Special attention was given to signal communications within the army reconnaissance structure. A special company was created and equipped with nine Realia-V signal sets that were able to cover a radius of about one and a half kilometers. With relay stations, this unit could communicate up to about forty kilometers. In addition to facilitating general communications for intelligence purposes, the unit was able to adjust artillery fire on the enemy, both at night and during the day. These radios also were useful in bringing in air strikes on designated targets.

From November 1983 to March 1984, this company was used to reconnoiter thirteen points on the main routes that the enemy used between bases in Pakistan and locations deep in Afghanistan. They detected 579 such movements in that period, 463 of them night movements.

Reconnaissance training of many commanders was rather poor, so that many, while estimating the situation and working out their decisions, depended on information provided by their higher headquarters or from the local populace. In both cases they discovered that the information provided was often worse than none at all. They did not try to use means at their own disposal for reconnaissance, although this certainly was possible. Often, this lack of personal initiative led to grave consequences. To overcome this obvious deficiency, the High Command established training courses of three days' duration, which included training in organizing ambushes. These helped to make the level of training of different reconnaissance units more uniform and proficient.

Combat actions in the mountains had to be able to adapt to many changing conditions. That is why tactical independence of small units was necessary, and why they had to obtain the best possible information on the enemy situation. Ambush operations were resorted to as a means of reconnaissance. Under conditions of mountainous terrain it was one of the most effective means that Soviet troops had for gaining information. The broken terrain, with its numerous natural obstacles and shelters, allowed our troops to enter a particular region secretly and set up ambush points. The enemy could not block Soviet troops from doing so because the sites were so numerous.

Since there were not many approach routes available for vehicles and horses, the enemy was forced to use the old caravan paths. This naturally facilitated accomplishment of combat missions for the Soviet troops when good information was available that the enemy was intending movement from one place to another. Setting up these ambushes, however, was not easy. As in any operation, it demanded of commanders and their subordinates careful preparation and a high level of professionalism.

Commanders learned that in mountainous terrain it was justified to lessen the distance between reconnaissance units and the main forces they were supporting since they were operating on foot. Commanders also decided to organize mobile observation posts to conduct surveillance over the entire route of advance of the main troop unit. This decision was fully justified in combat.

Locations for observation posts were chosen on the slopes of dominant terrain features, to make it possible to observe nearby heights and the entire length of ravines. To achieve this the posts were established in echelon at different altitudes. At night, some of the observation posts were moved from heights to lower elevations, since in the dark it was more convenient and effective to observe the heights from below.

As Soviet soldiers became more used to operating in combat in Afghanistan, they learned that they had to be equipped with whatever was necessary for their missions, particularly in the mountains. In addition to organic weapons and observation equipment, reconnaissance troops had to have at their disposal sufficient quantities of ammunition, food, medicine, water, camouflage clothing, special boots, and alpine equipment. They had to become masters of camouflage, and endure privation as the situation demanded.

Troops conducting reconnaissance were taking casualties at an unacceptable rate. These losses from enemy fire occurred because reconnaissance units had no snipers who could fire immediately at detected emplacements of the enemy. Also lacking were artillery and air observers. Artillery fire and air support would have been of great aid to reconnaissance troops that became engaged with enemy forces. So steps were taken to add necessary personnel and equipment to all units.

Eventually, artillery became very widely used in all types of combat in Afghanistan. Commanders of combined arms units took all steps necessary to ensure close and constant coordination with supporting artillery batteries. The goal was that no separate unit of at least platoon size was sent into combat without artillery available to them.

COMBAT USE OF ARTILLERY

Soviet forces have been pioneers in the use of artillery to support maneuver troops. Experience in the Great Patriotic War (World War II) showed the army that good artillery fire is indispensable in achieving combat goals. Despite this, when operations began in Afghanistan, there were grave deficiencies apparent in artillery employment. Officers of all grades simply did not know the tactics necessary to ensure timely and accurate fire when called for by infantry and armored troops. They had not learned their lessons well enough in peacetime training exercises, so they were not able to perform their jobs properly under the much greater stress of real combat.

About 90 percent of the requests for artillery fire came from troops faced with an aggressive enemy in unplanned situations. Under such circumstances, fire direction centers could not bring sufficient available artillery fire on enemy emplacements in a timely manner. To accomplish their missions, they tried to use air strikes as a substitute for artillery fire, when the latter was clearly more appropriate. Another large deficiency was that both artillery and air units expended huge amounts of munitions without discernible effect on the enemy. They felt, we suppose, that such an extravagant expenditure of expensive and scarce ordnance was beneficial to the morale of the supported troops. But in Afghanistan, a combat operation could last for up to ten days. The constant inefficient artillery and air support over such a long time wasted a lot of munitions and occasionally caused friendly casualties. What was needed was timely and accurate fire on observed enemy forces, not a general distribution of fire around an area where the enemy troops might or might not be situated.

Operations in Afghanistan were very fast moving. When an air landing was achieved by helicopter, the Soviet airborne troops needed immediate artillery support. This was rarely available. Why?

Effective artillery fire depends on many variables. Its accuracy is enhanced when fire direction centers are aware of up-to-date meteorological conditions. Such esoteric influences as humidity, wind velocity and direction, and good topographic maps must be considered by artillery planners if their fire is to be effective. Unfortunately, the maps available covered only about 25 percent of the land areas of the country. Added to this problem was a grave shortage of meteorological stations to give the artillery the information needed. But the units themselves were also guilty of poor technical performance in using their own equipment. And radio communications were a constant problem all through the war. Supported units had trouble communicating with the artillery and air force support means.

Another indirect fire weapons system was available to infantry units, the 82mm Podnos mortar. Since these mortars were available immediately to the infantry, they were effective in providing surprise fire on enemy positions in a timely manner. But although the mortars were an integral part of their own units, troops often called for support from distant artillery or air units. Statistics prove that this excellent mortar system was not used to its full capacity during the war. Trying to substitute artillery or air for the mortars caused loss of time and, in the end, poor results.

Official records show that only one artillery or air mission in four was successful. Two factors contributed to this, both related to reconnaissance: Often, information gained was basically unreliable and, many times, the information gained in the evening was delivered the following morning, too late to catch the enemy in their positions.

When reconnaissance information was accurate and available in a timely manner, the troops were able to perform their missions well with effective artillery and air support. From November 1983 to March 1984, some two hundred small-unit missions were concluded, many of them successfully. Afteraction reports say that false or outdated reconnaissance information was responsible for the failures reported.

When attacking hardened enemy positions, higher caliber weapons systems had to be used. The M-240 240mm mortar was the weapon of choice for this type of fire mission.

Another weapon, the Uragan rocket, proved to be extremely effective in a number of variations. This versatile rocket could be fired with a high-explosive fragmentation warhead, useful against personnel in the open, or to sow mines at long distances. In a typical operation against enemy troops in a village, about 40 percent of the initial rocket fire would be of the fragmentation variety. Later, when the enemy showed signs of pulling out, the rockets would be fired to lay mines to disrupt their movement out of the area. When firing at caves sheltering personnel and weapons systems, the high-explosive ammunition again was resorted to.

Ordinarily, one Uragan battery was assigned to a motor rifle division in combat. The battery fired in mass or by platoons as the fire mission indicated. In the latter case, the lieutenant commanding the platoon was responsible for everything to prepare for the fire mission: obtaining reconnaissance information, meteorological data, and other technical factors. He also had to coordinate with the maneuver element that he was supporting.

Sometimes, it was possible to adjust the fire of the Vasilyok 82mm mortar directly on the target. This weapons system was mounted on armored personnel carriers and therefore accompanied the troops near the target area where the enemy positions could be identified by the gunners.

Counterbattery fire against the enemy's artillery and mortars was a constant task. Their portable mortars and rocket launchers inflicted heavy losses on Soviet troops, particularly when they were occupying strong defensive positions. Their tactics involved surprise, firing only a short time from one position and then moving rapidly to an alternative site. They frequently bombarded Soviet troops early at night with concentrated fire for five or six minutes. After that the position was camouflaged and the crew withdrawn. If the crew was in no danger, the mortars or rocket launchers would be moved with them. They mounted these systems on vehicles and placed them under tents, so that it was difficult to detect them in time to bring effective fire against them. Soviet observers tried to locate them by the flash of the weapons. One tactic of the Soviets was to preplan fires in areas of suspected enemy concentrations. This proved to be more effective than a hurried adjustment on an enemy position that might well be evacuating.

Very seldom did the enemy in Afghanistan concentrate his forces in large numbers. Instead, he tended to employ small numbers in pinpoint-type emplacements—a mortar section or squad of ten men or so. Such small groups were scattered over a large area and had to be fought singly as separate targets. Therefore, the Soviet fire had to be extremely accurate to be of any value. Antitank guided missiles were often effective when a suitable target was identified. Helicopters using the Sturm-S missile were not very effective and thus were used only rarely. It is fair to say that great quantities of artillery shells, rockets, and mortar rounds were expended without as much effect as hoped.

We have alluded previously to the fact that the enemy was elusive and highly maneuverable, making him extremely difficult to detect and attack by fire. Timing was all-important, in that many precious minutes were lost in calling in tactical air and helicopter strikes. Frequently, their rockets and bombs hit positions where the enemy had been, not where he had moved in the interim. Poor training of commanders in target acquisition and the abnormal complexity of having to operate in Afghanistan's mountainous terrain contributed to this overall lack of success.

The forward air controller (FAC) was an important player in getting proper coordination between air assets and the maneuver elements. But since the FACs were on the ground attached to combat battalions, they frequently became casualties. Getting replacements for them was extremely difficult, so various company and battalion commanders began to train their own FACs from the troops available to them. Junior officers and noncommissioned officers were given this special training during stand-down periods between operations.

Soviet aviation was active and responsive, flying many sorties daily. On important days, pilots of front aviation flew up to four sorties; army helicopter crews sometimes flew as many as ten sorties. Aviation assets of all types were controlled centrally, and assets were assigned to strikes based on requests from the maneuver elements. Such requests were in written form if time permitted and oral under emergency situations. These, of course, had to be fully justified.

Radar was used to position combat aircraft in assigned missions. The enemy knew this and tried to attack radar posts whenever possible. This threat was constant, so that radar installations tended to be located within the perimeter of combat forces for protection. Sometimes, these positions were not the optimum sites the radar operators needed to achieve proper results. A larger problem that defied solution was the influence of the mountainous terrain and the frequent poor weather conditions. Sandstorms, sharp changes in temperature, and unforeseen shifts in atmospheric conditions proved deleterious to the functioning of the radar sets themselves.

OTHER COMBAT SUPPORT UNITS

Since the enemy did not possess an aerial threat, air-defense units attached to divisions were used almost entirely in ground support roles. This was apart from the air-defense radars discussed before. As with their infantry and artillery brothers, they were trained in the same type of training cycles, both for any possible air-defense missions and for their ground support task. In this latter mission, they had to be sufficiently alert to fire their weapons at enemy targets while en route. Each air-defense team had its own sector of responsibility along the route of advance. Air-defense command posts were in constant communication with their batteries and assisted in target detection and fire control.

Engineer elements were important to ground maneuver forces. Their missions included protective mine laying and removal of enemy minefields. Their special equipment was vital in clearing both natural and man-made obstacles. But, as with many armies, maneuver troops had to be able to perform engineer tasks themselves, because the engineers could not be everywhere at once. Special tasks assigned to engineer units included protection of pipelines and airfields. Engineer troops escorted companies having convoy protection duties so they could be on hand to remove mines emplaced in roads. Between 1980 and 1985, Soviet troops cleared almost 23,000 mines of all kinds and captured some 56,000 antitank and antipersonnel mines as well as 68 tons of explosives. Mines used by the enemy were mainly of Italian, British, American, Belgian, Swedish, and even Czechoslovakian manufacture.

During the same period, engineers laid 837 minefields consisting of about 91,000 antipersonnel mines. By helicopter, more than a million mines were placed, and by the aerial Vilyui system in 1983 and 1984 more than 1.7 million mines were laid in 429 minefields. Afghan troops laid some 200,000 mines over a five-year period.

Soviet forces were gravely hampered in their operations by the enemy's canny use of mines. They were laid on probable approach routes, particularly on roads and trails that were naturally difficult to negotiate. They put them everywhere, on bypasses and fords, deserted villages, water supply points, and, of course, on near approaches to enemy positions. The enemy's skillful use of mines made the Soviet high command change normal tactics and the structure of combat formations of columns.

Soviet combat actions in Afghanistan lasted for an excruciating ten years, with combat conditions severe in the extreme. Did either side gain overall success? The answer must be a qualified "no." Neither party achieved its goal. The Soviets were successful in preventing the Mujahidin from overthrowing the Afghan government, but were not able to suppress the rebellion. At a cost of many soldiers killed and more wounded, the result was inconclusive, with no glory brought to anyone.

Chapter 4

AFTER THE SOVIET TROOPS WERE GONE

INTERNATIONAL GUARANTEES

Shortly after Perez de Cuellar was elected the secretary general of the United Nations (UN) in January 1982, he appointed Diego Cordovez his deputy. In less than three months this prominent diplomat went to Kabul and then to Islamabad on a mission to promote negotiations to bring to an end the Soviet occupation of Afghanistan.

Beginning in 1982, Cordovez held forty-one discussions and a great number of meetings with Afghan, American, Pakistani, and Soviet officials and UN representatives, who took part in the various stages of the Geneva dialogue.

Cordovez used the results of his talks as a basis for a draft agreement, which read that the Soviet Union would withdraw its troops from Afghanistan at a date determined in the negotiations. Moscow gave a positive response in December 1982, about three weeks after Yuri Andropov* came to power. Andropov had private discussions with Pakistan's president, Zia ul-Haq, at Leonid Brezhnev's funeral. He assured the Pakistani leader of the "Soviet side's new flexible policy and its

---

*Andropov was the general secretary of the Communist party of the Soviet Union (1982–1983).

willingness to bring an early solution to the crisis." The only condition was that Pakistan had to stop its aid to the Mujahidin.

American journalists' interviews with the Pakistani leaders demonstrated an increasing disagreement between Islamabad and Washington concerning the UN propositions. President Zia ul-Haq announced on October 31 in Islamabad that Pakistan would support Cordovez's, plan "against our closest friend's advice. . . . We want a fair solution on our own initiative, since we know that political pressure may go along with a military one." The Pakistani foreign minister, Yaqub Khan, said in November, "We could bring the clock of history back to 1979. . . ."

Yaqub Kahn claimed that if the Soviet Union agreed to a rapid withdrawal from Afghanistan, Islamabad and Washington would be willing to provide their assistance during the pullout and help secure an end to the civil war. Andropov was also ready to start a diplomatic solution in Afghanistan. The facts that had been whispered about were officially admitted in the press: "Our men in Afghanistan are being killed by the rebels. The opposition is strong and experienced enough to effectively fight against the Soviet infantry and tanks in the country's mountainous terrain."

On the eve of the April round of talks, Cordovez and Perez de Cuellar had a meeting with Andropov, who made it clear that the Soviet Union was ready to take "certain steps" but doubted that Pakistan and the United States would back the UN proposal. Stressing the importance of the second part of the agreement, concerning the issue of noninterference, Andropov told de Cuellar that he was grateful to Cordovez for "realizing the importance of the issue for the Soviet Union." Cordovez later said that their hour-long discussion was focused entirely on the Afghan issue. Andropov finished his speech enumerating the reasons that gave impetus to the Soviet Union to seek an early solution to the Afghan conflict. "First," he said, "the conflict has affected Soviet relations not only with the West, but with other socialist countries, Arab countries, and Third World countries. Second, it has affected our home life, our policy, and economy."

As reported in the western press, the Soviet ambassador to Pakistan, Mr. Smirnov, officially reaffirmed that Moscow and Kabul were willing to negotiate a "time limit for the withdrawal of Soviet troops from Afghanistan."

But after Yuri Andropov was confined in a hospital in August 1983, Selig Harrison argues, Soviet diplomats did not do much to support the UN proposals. Cordovez turned in his draft agreement to Moscow and Washington, but there were no replies. The U.S. State Department made official mention only of a UN dialogue among the parties. Meanwhile, Soviet-American relations were going from bad to worse, especially after a Korean airliner was shot down in September 1983.

Now we can only regret that the United States and the Soviet Union failed to find a common ground in their attempts to resolve the Afghan crisis when the Soviet UN representative, Evstafiev, argued that in 1983 Andropov had an eight-month plan for a Soviet pullout. If Yaqub Khan had signed a bilateral agreement with Kabul, the plan could have been entered as its integral part.

It was only in 1988 that Soviet-American relations were sufficiently correct to work out the joint declaration on Afghanistan that played a most important role in the Soviet government's decision to withdraw its troops.

Two Stages and No Losses

Under the Geneva agreements, the Soviet Union was to finish its withdrawal from Afghanistan in nine months beginning May 15, 1988, with half of the Soviet contingent to be pulled out over the first three months. An international team under UN auspices was to supervise the withdrawal.

There were two routes of the Soviet withdrawal: via Kushka and via Termez. The transportation sequence was strictly observed. Between May 15 and August 1988, about 50,200 Soviet troops returned to Soviet territory from garrisons in Jalalabad, Ghazni, Gardez, Faizabad, Kunduz, Lashkargah, and Kandahar.

At the time of the Soviet troops' transit from Afghanistan, special blocking groups of troops secured the communication lines and placed fire on the regions of the Mujahidin's own live fire resources. The areas of night bivouacs were constantly lighted by Soviet aviation, ruling out a secret infiltration by the rebels. These measures helped keep losses at a minimum, preventing possible attacks by the opposition.

Some 212 correspondents were engaged in covering the withdrawal. They came from Austria, Britain, Italy, Spain, Canada, the United States,

Sweden, Finland, the Federal Republic of Germany (FRG), and Japan, as well as fifteen journalists from the Soviet Union. They escorted the Soviet troops to Kabul and from there to the Soviet state border. No censorship was imposed. They were provided every chance to give comprehensive coverage of the events.

Still, in one respect, the supervision mechanism created by the UN proved to be ineffective. As reported in the newspapers, the UN teams were not allowed free access in the opposition training centers in Pakistani territory.

After the first stage of the withdrawal had been completed, Soviet troops still remained in seven Afghan provinces. They concentrated their efforts on providing aid for Afghan armed forces in retaining important administrative centers, air bases, and communications, and supported the Afghan army in its struggle against the opposition in various regions of the country.

Once the withdrawal of the Soviet troops started, the armed opposition increased its pressure on the regime, intensifying its combat activities and stepping up its propaganda to demoralize the PDPA, the government, and the army. It undertook a series of operations to seize power in Kunar, Nangarhar, Paktia, Logar, Wardak, and Kandahar provinces. In response, government troops, supported by the remaining Soviet units, mainly aviation, conducted military operations against the rebels, thus restoring the balance of military-political control in Afghanistan.

It is noteworthy that the Afghan governmental leaders were most reluctant to allow their forces to engage in the struggle against the armed opposition during the final stage of the Soviet withdrawal. Their excuse was their desire to save their army for future struggles after the Soviet troops were gone. To hold back the rebels, they tried to use the units of the Fortieth Soviet Army, which had a wealth of combat experience, hoping to involve our troops in large-scale and long-lasting military operations, thus keeping them in Afghanistan for a longer time. More than once the Afghan leadership called on the Soviet government to suspend the troops' withdrawal, alleging that Pakistan and the United States violated the Geneva accords and that the armed opposition was building up its forces for a massive offensive.

The second stage of the Soviet withdrawal was orderly and practically without losses. The opposition with only a few exceptions did not try to stop the movement of Soviet troops from the beginning to the end. Neither did it try to stop the Afghan army from taking over the previously Soviet-held zones as well as support and security posts. It was only in southern Salang that force was used against the rebel Ahmed Shah Masud unit. The Afghan government and the Soviet military command in extensive talks with Ahmed Shah Masud tried to convince him to open a dialogue with the government, sign a protocol, and provide the protection of a vitally important highway. But a flat "no" came as a response. Moreover, he threatened that he would not permit government troops to enter southern Salang. His units blocked the road and opened fire the moment Afghan troops appeared. The Afghan troops counterattacked, supported by Soviet artillery units, resulting in the defeat of Masud's units. This allowed the Afghan troops to bring the region under government control.

As the Soviet troops were leaving for home, thousands of people gathered at the high bank of the Amu-Darya River to watch the armored vehicles moving along the bridge that connected the Soviet Union and Afghanistan. Lieutenant Alexei Sergachev, who began his career in Afghanistan as a private soldier, was in the first armored personnel carrier (APC).

The APC, with the Fortieth Army commander, Boris Gromov, was among the last in the column. General Gromov reported to the commander in chief of the Southern Command, Col. Gen. Nickolay Popov, that the withdrawal of Soviet troops from Afghanistan was complete.

Then, General Gromov saw his son, who had come to meet him, and they walked together over the remaining section of the bridge. His face was lined with immense tension and fatigue.

In Termez, General Gromov said to reporters, "This is the day millions of Soviet people have been waiting for. The nine-year-old war is over. . . ."

Soon the last armored vehicles, covered with dust and dented by shells and bullets, brought the officers of the staff operation group to Soviet soil. Now, one could say there was not a single Soviet soldier left on the other bank of the river.

There was still no peace on the Afghan side of the Amu-Darya, but deep in their hearts the soldiers hoped that some agreement would be found. They thought it was for the sake of that elusive peace that their comrades had shed their blood. It never occurred to them that they had been fighting against the Afghan people, who rose to defend their motherland, and that their military support for the Afghan government caused deeper split within the Afghan people. They were responsible for millions of the killed and wounded Afghans, not only the Mujahidin but civilians as well. The thousands of killed and crippled Soviet soldiers were a result of Soviet military interference in the home affairs of another country. But are the soldiers guilty of this? No, soldiers are the same anywhere; they are under orders from the politicians leading the country.

FACE TO FACE WITH THE MUJAHIDIN

The withdrawal of Soviet troops from Afghanistan brought about a dramatic change in the country's military-political situation. The government was facing a challenge from the opposition, which remained strong since economic and military aid from the United States, Pakistan, Iran, and China did not stop. It would seem that the odds were heavily against the government, giving the opposition a good chance to seize power. Both the Soviet leadership and the Najibullah government clearly realized this possibility. So, although Soviet troops were being withdrawn, considerable aid to the Afghan army was provided by the Soviet Union. Afghan authorities insisted that the Soviet Union provide for technical modernization of the Afghan armed forces, emphasizing the need for supplies of sophisticated weapons. The Kremlin could not afford to deny this request. However, as had happened before, the new supplies would not improve the overall quality of the Afghan army. A lion's share of the "resources" was useless because of a lack of specialists. The weapons, armaments, and vehicles were stored in warehouses. The majority of Afghan soldiers and officers did not know how to operate the sophisticated military equipment supplied by the Soviets.

Soviet military instructors, advisers to Afghan units, were supplied to provide training for the Afghan military, teaching them combat tactics, along with lessons learned on withstanding attacks by the rebels in the country's mountainous terrain. A report by the Soviet Defense Ministry Operation Group in Afghanistan of January 21, 1988, reads:

> To effectively withstand attacks by the opposition, we recommended to the Afghan leadership that large military units be concentrated to the extent possible in the most important places. Practical measures have been implemented. We believe it would be possible to hold Kabul, Herat, Kandahar, Gardez, Jalalabad, Khost, and the Kabul-Hairatan highway.

Measures are also being taken (before the Soviet withdrawal) to disband small garrisons to safeguard them and deprive the opposition of other occasions to triumph.

The country's leadership has at last realized the importance of undertakings designed to add to its power both in the central area and in the provinces. Local organizational work aimed at strengthening the nation has been started. Local council elections for the national assembly have been held. But everything is being done too slowly. The Afghan leadership until lately must have hoped the Soviet troops would not be withdrawn. There can hardly be any other explanation for the passivity observed in leaders at all levels.

Despite our repeated advice, the PDPA's leading role in everything is being unfittingly overemphasized, especially in the provinces. The multiparty system, introduced in the country, is not always taken into account. The government administrative apparatus does not enjoy enough power and thus plays a secondary role.

The People's Democratic Party of Afghanistan suffers from the same diseases, such as factionalism. They have not yet become overpowering, but the threat of internecine dissension, up to armed conflicts, is quite real. The dissension is based on contradictory feelings among the tribes and nationalistic elements as well as desires for vengeance.

A block of left-wing parties is taking shape, but it holds out little hope; the right time has been missed.

Under the circumstances, numerous requests from Afghan leaders were swiftly and completely fulfilled. Intensive training in Soviet military colleges and academies was provided for Afghan officers and students. Due to extensive military and other supplies coming from the Soviet Union, ample reserves of material resources able to last for months were stored in key Afghan regions. Cantonments and support bases, earlier occupied by Soviet units, passed to the Afghans. There were increased supplies to meet the needs of the population: foodstuffs, consumer goods, various necessities, and building materials. To a great extent, due to this aid, the country's vital activities were maintained. According to estimates of economists, spending for this aid amounted to more than 2 billion rubles during the single year 1989.

This great assistance provided by the Soviet Union to Afghanistan unfortunately failed to bring about the desired result. This happened not only because of errors in running the country and disruption of economic ties caused by the long civil war; to a great extent, it occurred because of the continuous struggle for power within the party and its leadership.

The leaders of the Khalq wing of the People's Democratic Party of Afghanistan never stopped taking credit for causing the revolution and doing more than their share in fighting on the battlefields. Moreover, they charged that the Parchamists, with the help of the Soviet Union, usurped power both in the country and in the party. The Khalqists accused the Soviet Union of giving one-sided support to the Parchamists. The Soviet military presence helped to control open advances by the Khalqists, thus serving as a reconciling factor. However, a secret struggle between the wings was going on.

The attempt undertaken by the former Afghan defense minister, Shah Nawaz Tanay, on March 6, 1990, in Kabul to forcibly overthrow President Najibullah is yet another indication of this rivalry. Although the mutiny failed to change the general situation in the country, it was followed by political instability in the country. As it grew, so did the number of President Najibullah's adversaries within his own party, both in Afghanistan and elsewhere. The opposition was provided with a good excuse to continue its military pressure on Kabul, and intensify its activities in other regions of the country.

This attempt at a coup d'état had to affect the army. Inevitable repressions against the activists of Tanay's plot aggravated the complicated relations between the army's Khalqists and Parchamists. The repressions strengthened oppositional attitudes of some officer personnel against President Najibullah and his associates. The number of deserters from the army increased, with some units even joining the opposition. In March–June 1990 the number of units that changed sides increased, especially in the troops defending Khost, Jalalabad, and some strategic communication centers. There was a threat that some garrisons where Tanay's supporters were strongest might abandon their loyalty to the government. All of this weakened the Afghan armed forces.

At the same time, a swift and resolute suppression of the military plot demonstrated President Najibullah's ability to act in critical situations, the strength of his regime and his capability of withstanding the opposition without the support of Soviet troops. The situation seemed to develop into a stalemate: The opposition was not able to overthrow the regime, and the latter, being on the strategic defensive, was unable to defeat the rebel military units. Further events depended on both sides' readiness to compromise and cooperate in bringing about peace and stability to the country. Even if the "irreconcilables" were to come to power, the war still would not end, since the rebels themselves are disunited. They are nonhomogeneous and do not enjoy support all over the country. It is not by chance that their units are fighting not only against government troops, but against each other, either to stabilize their areas of control or to expand them.

Much depends on Soviet-American relations. As long as the United States and the Soviet Union continue to support the two sides, the war in Afghanistan is unlikely to end in the near future.

ALONG THE PATH TO RECONCILIATION

Afghan President Najibullah was in the Soviet Union in September 1990 on a short working visit. In an interview he spoke for reconciliation with all opposition forces, stressing the need for a political settlement that included several stages.

As reported in Pravda, September 17, 1990, President Najibullah gave the following statement:

> We agree that there should be a transitional period, which would begin with an inner Afghan dialogue and continue until a new government is formed. A joint commission must be formed that would include representatives of all political forces united for a peaceful settlement. The task of the commission would be to provide for holding new elections, distributing UN supplies, and securing the return of refugees. Armed units of the Afghan army and the opposition could be attached to it to ensure security. The commission would work out a new law on elections and a new constitution to be adopted by a *Loya jirga* ["people's assembly"]. Until a new government is elected by the parliament, the present government structures must remain in power.

To bring this policy of national reconciliation into being, the Afghan military-political leadership undertook a series of steps aimed first at resolving various social problems, promoting dialogue with the opposition, and creating a basis for civil peace. The process of forming a new political system began, designed to ensure the democratization and liberalization of internal political life, and to create favorable conditions for the reconstruction of the national economy. A very significant component of the state political structure has been revived, namely the Afghan parliament. A law on the activities of political parties has been adopted and a system for holding general elections on a multiparty basis worked out.

Reform in the People's Democratic Party of Afghanistan was a political event of major importance. The second PDPA Congress, held in June 1990, considered the renovation of the party. It took steps to renounce its monopoly on power and to establish new relationships with other parties as well as state and public organizations. The new program calls for progress in the development and restoration of the economy and culture, considering national and Islamic values to be the party's top priorities. The congress decided to change the name of PDPA to the Watan (Homeland) Party. The clause of the constitution proclaiming the party's single leading role was removed.

A new government has been formed on democratic principles. Twelve of the thirty-six ministers are members of the Homeland Party; the rest belong to other parties and organizations or are unaffiliated.

The Afghan Peace Front, a new organization created on the basis of the National Front, plays an important role in the overall national reconciliation policy. To unite all national patriotic forces, both inside Afghanistan and those temporarily abroad, and attract them to building a new and independent Afghanistan are seen as major goals of the Peace Front.

The leadership of the Republic of Afghanistan is striving to broaden the policy of national reconciliation and involve wider sections of the opposition in the process. President Najibullah's decree on the return of the confiscated property to former owners is expected to play a major role. Real estate and personal property—land, factories, trading houses and stores, currency, and stocks and bonds—are being returned.

To develop this program, the government and the Homeland Party initiated a series of measures designed to work out mutually acceptable compromises with the opposition, a mechanism for a political settlement and setting up coalition power structures. Afghan leaders proposed to the opposition a scheme for a political settlement in several stages. It stipulates a cease-fire and truce until a transitional period starts. During the transitional period, it is planned to promote an inner-Afghan dialogue and to convene a national conference that will set up a Joint Coordination Committee (JCC), with all the parties involved in the conflict represented. Members of the JCC will be allowed to retain control over their territories and their administration. The Afghan government expressed its readiness to give the opposition the functions of some ministries, whose activities would coincide with the JCC's goals. The second stage envisages the beginning of UN-supervised preparations for general elections. Truly free elections, which will determine the places that different political forces would have in the state's parliamentary structure, are expected to be held at the third stage. Being well aware of the difficulties that the first stage may present, the government suggested conducting a referendum on the issue of a cease-fire in all regions of the country, whether under governmental control or not.

The talks that President Najibullah held in Switzerland in December 1990 with former King Zahir Shah's representatives and the opposition forces, the Alliance of the Seven,* were a major step by the Afghan leadership in seeking mutually acceptable compromises. The talks resulted in agreements aimed at an early cease-fire. The Afghan government made it clear that it was ready to make considerable concessions, including giving up military supplies from the Soviet Union and reducing the stocks of weapons, provided that the United States stopped sending similar supplies to the Mujahidin. Other ways to attract foreign diplomatic forces and international legal bodies to promote a compromise in Afghanistan are being studied.

Political activities of the Afghan government and the Homeland Party are accelerating either to neutralize the rebels or attract them to the side of the state. They actively are courting opposition field commanders, chiefs of the tribes, religious leaders, leaders of the ethnic

---

*An alliance of Islamic militants within the Mujahidin in Pakistan composed of seven most influential Sunnite parties. This group is generally in opposition to the similar Alliance of the Eight, which is Shiite in religious orientation and operates within or on the border of Iran.

communities, and rank-and-file members of armed groups. The government made an appeal to all opposition commanders acting within the country to engage in direct negotiations to find any possible ways to stop the bloodshed. The government agreed to provide full independence, both political and economic, within the regions under their control; it is also ready to provide material-technical aid to the regions.

These initiatives of the Afghan leadership to bring an early end to the civil war have had an effect on their rivals. Attitudes on both sides in favor of stopping the fighting are gaining momentum. Out of 6,000 units and rebel groups within the country, about 3,000 are biding their time, 1,500 have entered into negotiations, and some 700 units have signed an agreement to give up the armed struggle. A hundred units have actually joined the government forces.

President Najibullah's political actions to develop a policy of national reconciliation are accompanied by moves to restore the country's economy. The government has chosen a liberal course, setting up a permanent commission, attached to the Council of Ministers. It will deal with internal and external investments in the private sector. One of the main tasks of the commission is to support free enterprise through the distribution of state orders and to accommodate projects, approved by the government, with loans. In 1990, for example, the commission underwrote more than thirty economic projects throughout the country. These included chemical and food industries, agriculture, building-materials production, and mass media.

Much attention is being given to the economic development of the northern regions of the country, which are rich in natural resources and have a skilled labor force and traditional trade links with the Soviet Union. Exports from this region will be increased, and will serve as a basis for heavy industry there and in other provinces.

The republic's overall production, despite many difficulties, is functioning at a minimal but stable level to satisfy the country's vital needs.

In the military-political sphere effective armed counteraction to the opposition is of major importance. Attempts undertaken in 1990 to improve the armed forces' efficiency and boost the morale of the personnel proved to be successful. Government troops have frustrated the rebel units' plan to take over Kabul and other administrative centers. The country's armed forces control the main communications links and the vital regions of Afghanistan.

A pronounced tendency toward normalization, in spite of the fighting going on, stimulates the return of Afghan refugees. Since early 1990 more than 100,000 refugees reemigrated to Afghanistan. The UN High Commission for Refugees estimated that another 40,000 Afghan families left their refugee camps in Pakistan in 1990. Even if the military-political situation does not change, some 250,000 people, experts say, have come home. A similar process is under way on the Afghan-Iranian border, with about 3,000 refugees crossing it monthly. All in all, since the start of the national reconciliation policy, by early 1991 more than 300,000 people had returned to Afghanistan.

Despite definitely positive changes in the country during 1990, the government failed to reach the desired improvement in the military-political situation. The national reconciliation policy has not yet yielded tangible results because it lacks an effective mechanism in its realization. Implacable attitudes on the rival sides caused by the political polarization of the Afghan society still persist. The bulk of the opposition adamantly refuses to compromise with the present government, making its resignation a precondition for a dialogue. The government's drive to impose its own terms does not help in promoting civil peace in Afghanistan. The opposition will not accept its terms based on an unequal distribution of seats in future coalition bodies of power.

The system of state power in the Republic of Afghanistan remains unstable despite all the measures tried to strengthen it. The development of new control structures has resulted in protracted delay. The new Afghan parliament, in fact, has had its lawmaking powers curtailed, and is really only a consultative body, its public role being quite ineffective. Local authorities are inoperative and are deeply affected by corruption. Clan and local interests take precedence over those of the state.

The Homeland Party is in a deep crisis. Its shaky political and public status and its hasty retreat from monopoly power have weakened its position. Stratification and inner discord continue to be characteristic of the party. The factional rivalry between the Khalqists and Parchamists is dominating. New factions, representing the already-known political trends (Amin's and Taraki's supporters) as well as fresh ones formed by new party leaders, continue to emerge. Judging by the reports of local observers, the party apparatus is corrupted, paralyzed by bureaucratism, and enjoys low credibility both within its own ranks and the population at large.

The bloc of the left-democratic forces, weakened by both inner-party dissension and the fight for broader representation in state bodies, has failed to play an important role in the policy of national reconciliation.

The country's defense system is not united. This includes the army, state security, interior and territorial troops, revolutionary defense units, tribal volunteer units, and the left-democratic bloc's armed units. The government does not have a unified organizational structure with singular command and control. The morale of many units is shattered.

The antigovernment opposition that has rejected the national reconciliation policy and pushed for further confrontation remains a meaningful military and political force. It is well manned and is able to wage war throughout almost the entire country. The total strength of the rebel groups is more than 180,000 people. Blocking the main highways and taking over large administrative centers, the opposition leaders try to narrow the territory under government control and eventually crush the existing regime. The regions bordering on Pakistan are in the worst danger. The cities of Kandahar, Gardez, Jalalabad, and some central provinces have been in a state of siege.

The occupation by the Mujahidin of Khost, a large Afghan power center, in March 1991 was a great military-political victory scored by the opposition. As the western press described, it is a natural step on the road to taking full control of the country.

What allowed the Mujahidin to win such an outstanding victory? As has already been mentioned, the opposition has remained disunited throughout the Afghan war. Internecine dissension often grew into protracted battles with heavy weaponry. They would subside, then flare up anew. However, since early 1991 more agreement among the Mujahidin seems evident, so the opposition against the Najibullah regime has more coherence than before, if not a united front. The occupation of Khost, which was defended by a 10,000-man garrison with a deeply echeloned circular defense, containing tanks, artillery, and combat aviation, is a good indication of this.

Some circles in Kabul tend to think that the main reason for the defeat at Khost was a massive four-direction offensive by the rebels supported by Pakistani artillery, and the use of armor to break through the defense in a narrow area. Some allege that treason was a factor. Still, the primary reason, as more and more Kabul officials have come to realize, is that this time the Mujahidin were coordinated as never before. They acted under a single plan, under the single command of D. Haqqani.

The Bakhtar news agency reported that representatives of the U.S. CIA and Pakistani military advisors went out of their way to unite the Afghan opposition. The U.S. ambassador in Pakistan, R. Oakley, along with high-ranking Pakistani military, headed by the chief of Military Intelligence, Major General Durrani, were reported to have participated in a series of talks with the leaders of the "seven," at which they in strong terms recommended that they cut short the feud among the rebel groups and their commanders.

Meanwhile, according to the Pakistani press, a special White House envoy, P. Thomsen, held a series of meetings with the leaders of major parties and field commanders. He also met several times with the leader of the so-called provisional government, Mojaddedi. These initiatives resulted in a meeting of the leading field commanders in Peshawar. An all-Afghan council of field commanders was set up at this meeting. Its main objective was to create a single front in the struggle against President Najibullah, and to coordinate joint actions over the period of the spring-summer military campaign of 1991. A number of committees (military, political, security) were formed to make the plan operational.

One of the field commanders, M. Anwar, stated that it was at a session of the all-Afghan council of field commanders that the operation against Khost was planned. Actions of about fifty of the attacking units, more than 15,000 men, were coordinated precisely.

At the same time, the Afghan mass media as well as western radio stations continued to argue that Mujahidin unification is only temporary. The theory is that it took place to again demonstrate to the West and some Arab countries that the Mujahidin still remained a real force, consequently needing larger amounts of financial aid. Newspapers, radio, and television daily carry reports of fighting among the rebels. In fact, there are clashes in opposition ranks, as the Afghan Interior Ministry confirms. Still, one cannot fail to observe a considerable consolidation within the Mujahidin. Many issues of discord between the armed units of Sunnites and Shiites belonging to different parties have been settled.

Opposition units regularly fire missiles against the capital and main administrative centers of the country. This is detrimental to the government and to a great extent undermines its authority. Government troops have a difficult time defending Kabul, Nangarhar, Kandahar, Paktia, and other provinces. The opposition continues to launch recurrent large-scale attacks against large cities, including the capital, Kabul.

Terrorist acts on the main communication lines as well as acts of direct and indirect sabotage in the towns disrupt traditional economic ties between urban and rural areas. Operations in provinces, districts, and rural areas are especially important to the opposition, aimed at bringing about an atmosphere of chaos, with food and commodity shortages, as they cause discontent with the regime.

One of the main objectives of the opposition in 1990 was to upset the Salam ("peace") program. Salam is a program of international aid for Afghanistan, which among other things promotes the return of Afghan refugees. In order to frustrate the work of the UN units directly involved in implementing the program, one of the most irreconcilable leaders of the Alliance of the Seven, G. Hikmatiyar, ordered the formation of a special terrorist group, the Afghan International Jihad. The group organizes terrorist acts against the columns of Afghan refugees on their way home, thereby exerting psychological pressure on the UN and representatives of other international organizations. In addition, a large-scale antirepatriation propaganda campaign has been launched. Special groups equipped with technical propaganda capabilities are in place in the refugee camps in Pakistan. Those who want to return to their motherland are classified as "traitors to the *jihad*" and "friends of the Russians," and are threatened with severe punishment.

Western observers explain the tactic of disrupting the process of the Afghan refugees' repatriation by concluding that it may undermine the social basis of the counterrevolution and deprive the opposition of people and material resources. Moreover, rebel leaders fear that the return of the refugees may eventually become a foundation for national reconciliation and help set up a credible coalition leadership.

The opposition skillfully combines its armed struggle with subversive propaganda, attempting to discredit the present party-state structure. The leaders of the opposition decided in 1990 to intensify their ideological activity inside Afghanistan. Special centers, where ideologists are being trained, have been established in Iran and Pakistan. Their subversive propaganda is designed to discredit both the country's present leadership and the policy of national reconciliation. By all available means the opposition is promoting the idea that the Kabul regime is doomed. They do everything possible to cast slurs upon the government and the Homeland Party, insisting that it is unable to solve the problems that Afghanistan is facing. Government officials, party functionaries, and military personnel are put under massive psychological pressure.

We should mention that the propaganda campaign is organized very skillfully. Knowing the people well, the Mujahidin appeal to their strong religious beliefs, thus having a great impact on the Afghan population. The inflexibility of official indoctrination combined with blunders by local authorities make things even worse.

During 1990, the political activity of the Afghan opposition "provisional government" in Pakistan intensified. Preparatory work to hold a Loya Jirga in the opposition-controlled areas was especially important to them. The opposition expects the jirga to elect a new government to run the occupied areas until President Najibullah is deposed. New structures within the local authority are being energetically formed. They expect to elect some 2,170 deputies. A special committee is in charge of achieving consensus on the idea of setting up a "coalition government" among the various Mujahidin groups. There are regular consultations with field commanders and the opposition organizations in Iran that belong to the Party of Islamic Unity.

However, serious contradictions persist within the opposition. Accord, for example, had not been reached between the traditionalists and fundamentalists as to the future of Afghanistan. The fundamentalist parties are for the creation of a supercentralized theocratic state; the traditionalists support the idea of returning to prerevolution times. There is still dissension between the Sunnite Alliance of the Seven in Pakistan and the Shiite Party of Islamic Unity based in Iran. Confrontation among units belonging to different parties has not calmed down completely.

The military confrontation in Afghanistan continues to cause great concern in the world. The United Nations is seeking ways of stopping the military conflict and restoring peace and normal life for all the people. There is a movement in the Soviet Union, the United States, and the Islamic Republic of Iran to revise their policies in Afghanistan. China too has decreased greatly its involvement in the conflict. But there is no unanimity yet in various military and political circles in Pakistan.

Observers believe that the present presents good situation prospects to resolve the Afghan conflict with the help of world opinion. The forty-fifth session of the UN General Assembly passed a resolution on this issue, calling for a comprehensive political settlement, an end to all combat actions in Afghanistan, and the provision of necessary controls to normalize the situation. The UN has called on the rival sides to start negotiations and has volunteered to mediate at the talks. A common Soviet-American approach to the problem of a settlement has been helpful in this regard.

At the talks between former Soviet Foreign Minister Shevardnadze and American Secretary of State Baker, held in Houston, Texas, in December 1990, it was concluded that elections in Afghanistan were essential. A provisional body is expected to be set up to organize the elections, to be held under UN supervision. More importantly, the Soviets and Americans agreed to stop arms supplies to the rival sides.

Summing up, the withdrawal of Soviet troops from Afghanistan failed to resolve the Afghan crisis. The war goes on there, causing many casualties among common people. The government in general is managing to control the situation in the country, while discord within the opposition prevents the rebels from seizing power at this time. The Afghan leadership continues to seek ways for a peaceful settlement while military measures are still being pursued. Today, any great changes in the situation hardly seem likely. Nevertheless, the political process within the opposition movement and international efforts by the concerned parties may eventually help solve the Afghan problem.

What circumstances can allow a settlement in Afghanistan? A revision of Soviet and western support to both Kabul and the opposition is one of them. As we investigate details of the Soviet aid supplied after the troops had left, current officials choose not to elaborate about it. However, the Soviet press reported in March 1991 that the Soviet Union was ready to provide extra aid worth $300 million to Kabul. The aid finally included grain supplies of 400,000 tons and up to 450,000 tons of fuel. We suspect that the uncontrolled inflow of such Soviet aid is not being used effectively in Afghanistan. Who cares to estimate the share of the aid that is being eventually pocketed by crafty dealers without reaching the people who really needed it?

Finally, another nagging problem is the endless Soviet aid to Kabul in weaponry. It is true that the Soviet military presence is over, but

military aid continues to arrive in Afghanistan, bringing no real results. Not only because the opposition gets its share of aid from the
West, it is most important to realize that the roots of the conflict lie
in the national psyche that the Soviet side refuses to see, remaining
the prisoner of old stereotypes. But no regime can survive with its power
being economically, politically, and morally exhausted. To our thinking,
it would be much wiser to use Soviet diplomacy to a greater extent to
stop all military supplies to the warring sides. One may say that we
are adhering to signed agreements, but the Soviet Army came to Afghanistan also in compliance with an agreement. Still, to the credit
of Soviet politicians and diplomats, they did manage to convince the
Afghan leadership that it was no longer feasible to keep the Soviet
troops in the country, allowing the Geneva accords to become a reality. The same can be done concerning the supply of weapons, provided that the other side does the same. The issue of Soviet aid has
moral and economic aspects too. It cannot go on forever, especially
now when the Soviet Union has been plunged into many deep crises
whose roots can be traced partially to the Afghan syndrome. In fact,
the Soviet Union we have known and served faithfully has ceased to
exist, replaced by a confederation of separate independent states. In
size and strength the Russian Republic seems to us dominant, particularly
since it has succeeded to the U.N. Security Council seat formerly occupied
by the U.S.S.R. It would seem that at this writing, Mr. Boris Yeltsin
has inherited the knotty problem of Afghanistan.

Chapter 5

CONCLUSION

When Babrak Karmal* arrived in the Soviet Union in 1987, having been ousted from office in his country, he was asked by newsmen what he thought of the Soviet military intervention in Afghanistan. He replied half-jokingly: "If Soviet troops had not entered our country, the world would never have heard of Afghanistan."

There is some truth in this remark. After Soviet troops came to Afghanistan, the world community seemed suddenly to have discovered that country. People began to be interested in its history, its domestic and foreign policies, and the circumstances that led to the April revolution and to the Soviet military intervention. And this interest has not diminished even today. The reason for this is the extraordinary nine-year war fought by Soviet troops on Afghan soil, a war that has come to be known as the Afghan syndrome.

What are we to think of what happened in Afghanistan during those nine years?

Afghanistan was, and still is, a very poor country, probably one of the poorest in the world. Its political system is hopelessly obsolete,

---

*Member of the People's Democratic Party of Afghanistan and head of the Afghan government from 1979 to 1986.

and this has acted as a brake on the country's development. Amanullah Khan was aware of this back in the 1920s. And Zahir Shah, the last king of Afghanistan, understood this and had tried to carry out some reforms. What happened in April 1978 was probably inevitable; the conditions in the country were ripe for such a turn of events. And whichever political group should come to power in the future, April 1978 will undoubtedly be seen as an unavoidable and even progressive event in the country's history. And it was so regarded by honest, thoughtful Afghans at that time. They had hoped and believed that the revolution would give a fresh impetus to the country's development. They supported the new regime.

But instead of broadening its social base, the new leadership adopted policies that alienated the people of entire social groups. In a highly devout country, it suppressed religious worship and dealt harshly with the clergy. Many religious figures joined the opposition camp and were often its most active members. Many of them were highly respected personages among the Afghans, and their prestige became still greater after they had been turned into martyrs as a result of the repressive policies toward them carried out by the new regime.

Amin and Karmal also managed to alienate the largest portion of the population, the peasantry, by their "agrarian reform," which did not in the least benefit these people. War destroyed the irrigation system; the fields were mined. Driven by a feeling of hopelessness, large numbers of peasants followed their own leaders, left the country, and soon found themselves fighting against the government.

The new regime might have found support in the country's armed forces, but the military was in disarray because of the factional struggle within the People's Democratic Party of Afghanistan. Both factions, the Parchamists and the Khalqists, tried to get the army to take sides. The result was that the army's combat efficiency was undermined.

Leading members of the Afghan intelligentsia began leaving the country. So did businessmen and merchants, taking their financial resources with them. The country became poorer, intellectually and economically. Many of those who went abroad refused to return to their homeland, despite pleas and incentives.

The Soviet Union had long had political and economic ties with Afghanistan, and had close contacts with the new leaders of that country.

It could have tried to prevent a split in Afghan society by political means, to bring about, through its good offices, a reconciliation of the opposing sides. It could have conducted a more flexible foreign policy. It could have helped to uphold the independence and sovereignty of Afghanistan and, what is most important, to preserve its friendly, good-neighborly relations with that country. Regrettably, the Soviet leadership decided to resort to military force, expanding the problem rather than solving it.

Probably none of the Soviet leaders who made the decision to give military support to the People's Democratic Party of Afghanistan, which had seized power in that country, could have foreseen the economic and moral damage their act was to inflict on the Soviet Union itself. Some people in the Soviet Union, especially in military circles, even now try to justify this act, if they do not exactly approve of it. Their view is that the Soviet Union could not have turned a deaf ear to the call for help of its "Afghan class brothers," that it had gone into Afghanistan with the best of intentions to save that country from its headlong fall into the abyss. It was such reasoning that prevented the Soviets, in 1979, from becoming aware of the pain and suffering that the Afghan people were experiencing. The Soviets had not yet learned the lessons of their own history, especially that of the years of the Hitlerite invasion (1941–1945). In 1979 they rather thoughtlessly accepted their politicians' assertions that sending troops into its neighboring country was a necessary, if difficult, decision. Even today some Soviet politicians argue that if the Soviets had not sent troops into Afghanistan, the Americans would have come there with their rockets. But this argument is unsound. If the United States were to have sent its rockets or troops to Afghanistan, it would have had to reach an agreement on this with the Afghan government. But there was no possibility of such an agreement then, as there is no such agreement today. Afghanistan has adhered to its traditional policy of nonalignment. It did not need any special attention from the Soviet Union or the United States. Furthermore, its history shows that it did not particularly like the Iranians or the Pakistanis. But the moment Soviet troops entered that country the West began pouring in money. According to western press reports, between 1980 and1985 U.S. aid alone amounted to $500 million, compared to years before when the United States had given no aid to Afghanistan at all. By May 1989, noted the *Financial Times* (July 12, 1989), this aid had reached some $2 billion. So began the competition. Who gave more, the USSR or the United States?

The Afghan war laid a heavy burden on the Soviet economy. Will we ever be able to count the total losses suffered by the Soviet Union in that war? Just the cost of delivering military and civilian goods to Afghanistan during the years that the Soviet troops were in that country, according to official Soviet figures, came to 60 billion rubles, at least $2.4 billion.

And what about the Soviet Union's loss in world prestige? The use of force is outmoded in the civilized world. The Soviets themselves helped to bring about this attitude, having so loudly and persistently condemned the military ventures of others. The antiwar wave now rocked the Soviets' own boat. And what about the human losses? Soviet losses in the war from 1979 to 1989 were 13,833 killed, 49,985 wounded, and 330 missing.

These are the aftermaths of the Afghan war: the heavy drain on the Soviet economy, the decline of the country's prestige in the world, distrust of their government on the part of the Soviet people, tens of thousands killed and wounded in action, invalids on the streets, and continued bloodshed in Afghanistan. Only a madman could try to justify all this by referring to certain high ideals and goals.

Events such as the Afghan war not only have negative consequences that are immediately apparent. They live on for decades in the memories of people and influence the actions of whole generations. They leave their imprint on history. And the most remarkable thing is that, for the Soviets, the negative consequences are interwoven with positive, even progressive ones. Now, let us take a look at these positive results of the Afghan syndrome.

Consider the United States and the Vietnam War. It has been said that after that war the voices of many reasonable, sensible people were heard in that country. But of course there have always been such people in that country, only nobody then wanted to hear what they had to say. What the Afghan war did to the Soviet people was to make them become more aware of their own problems. It is possible that if it were not for the Afghan war there would have been no perestroika, or perestroika would have begun in the next century. Probably the first real breakthrough of *glasnost* came when Mikhail Gorbachev was asked to tell the truth about the Afghan war. And was not the East-West rapprochement, and in particular the drawing together of the Soviet Union and the United States after 1988, not a result of the Afghan syndrome? During the Persian Gulf crisis, the world's nations, including the Soviet Union, stood together. Here, too, one may recall the Afghan lesson.

Mankind has become more determined to resist injustice and the use of force. It has become more civilized, more compassionate. Evidence of this is the current humanitarian aid given by the West to the now independent republics of the old Soviet Union and other countries as well as to nations suffering from outside aggression or international dictatorship.

Of course, in speaking of the positive results of the Afghan syndrome, we are not at all condoning the Afghan war or slurring over its tragic, even dangerous, consequences. Take, for example, the veterans of the Afghan war. These "Afgantsi" now make up quite a large social force.

They were about eighteen years of age when they were thrown into the war in Afghanistan. They were told that they would be fighting for the happiness of the Afghan people. But later they realized that their opponents on the battlefield were also Afghans, who were ready to lay down their lives for their own cause.

They were told that they were defending their homeland. Yet at home they were laughed at and advised to take off the medals they were wearing.

They displayed valor on the battlefield. They fought, so they were assured, for justice and the happiness of all. But when they returned home they were met with indifference and acts of injustice. They even became a source of irritation as they hobbled along on their crutches and went about seeking truth and justice. For by doing so they were violating the rules of the game played by a society that had buried its conscience.

Deceived, seared by the flames of battle, and neglected by the society that had sent them into a war fought on alien soil for alien ideals, these Afgantsi are reaching maturity, and the country's destiny will be in the hands of their generation. At the moment they are not organized; they are not subordinated to anyone. But what if some fanatic extremist should get hold of them? What if someone pursuing dubious ends should decide to have this "Afghan grenade" at his disposal?

The "Afghan generation" missed the time when they should have been in colleges and universities improving their capabilities. They were abruptly cast into the abyss of severe trial in a hard war. And when they came home, they were made to feel like outsiders. They were confused in trying to decide what to do in order to start leading a normal civilian life. For many of them it seems that the war has not yet ended. It followed them home, plaguing them as they tried to adapt to a new life. And for some, the full horrors of war have only lately become apparent. These included the disabled, the mothers who lost their sons, and men whose wives had left them after they became invalids while fighting in Afghanistan.

They weren't greeted as heroes when they came home. Even during the time of Stalin, who did not care at all in what miserable conditions the soldiers returning from the war in 1945 might live, there was no such hostility toward the war veterans as there has been toward the Afgantsi. True, in those days the prisoners of war and the soldiers, who not of their own will found themselves in places such as Yugoslavia or Greece where they joined the guerrilla fighters against Fascism and were regarded as heroes for their courage and valor, were sent straight to the concentration camps after they returned home. Stalin was afraid that they, having seen how people lived in those countries, should come to think unfavorably of socialism and of the regime he headed.

But what was the Soviet leadership afraid of in connection with the Afghan war? That Soviet servicemen would compare unfavorably the conditions at home with those in impoverished Afghanistan? Here the old way of thinking prevailed once again. And this meant recourse to hypocrisy, ruthlessness, and immoral and antidemocratic practices, which had in fact become part of state policy and largely influenced social attitudes.

Perestroika of course has introduced many new ideas and attitudes into Soviet society. People have become more democratic-minded, more open, freed from many former prejudices. The Afgantsi now enjoy all the benefits of war veterans, although, like the rest of society, they are far from being well-off.

But with all the acuteness of the Soviets' social and economic crises, and despite the introduction of reforms by Mikhail Gorbachev, the Soviets cannot yet say that the "Afghan syndrome" is fully understood. The real truth about the Afghan war has not yet been told. The Soviets still do not have a complete picture of what happened and why it happened and what the consequences are. What they have instead is a heap of unconnected facts: the talk about internationalist obligations and about the necessity of sending Soviet troops into Afghanistan; the political assessment of the war made by the USSR Supreme Soviet; the life of the Afgantsi; and the classified research conducted by military experts who viewed the Afghan theater of war as a training ground. Instead of living history there are particular interpretations of isolated events. The Afghan war is but one more crack in the foundation of the old Soviet society. Who stands to gain from such a state of affairs? Many, it seems.

It is a fact that both the "right" and the "left," the new political parties and social organizations, are trying to use the Afgantsi for their own ends, to exploit their strength, their status, and their feelings of anger and bitterness in their political games.

And then many of those who were actively involved in the dispatch of Soviet troops to Afghanistan are still alive and have in fact been promoted. Obviously they would not want to have all the circumstances related to the war investigated and become known, since this would turn public opinion against them.

Of course, time passes. And as the years go by passions will subside, different ideas will find their proper place in a more harmonious pattern, and what is superfluous and meaningless will be left out. People whose views seem irreconcilable now will come together and work toward a common goal. Our illusions and mistakes, our defeats and victories will all be given their due, their proper place in history, by those who will come after us, just as we have inherited and come to terms with the revolutions and wars conducted by those who preceded us. Time is the best judge.

But for the sake of our children and our grandchildren it is necessary that we should learn as much as we can of the truth of the Afghan war now. We need to understand the Afghan syndrome today to be able to prevent the use of force by the leaders of other countries, by the Saddam Husseins of the world who covet the territories of other nations.

It is to this end that this book has been written.

Appendix A

GEOGRAPHY

———————

The Republic of Afghanistan is a mountainous country. The average height of the territory is 900 to 1,200 meters above sea level. Afghanistan comprises an area of 655,000 square kilometers, with a border 5,421 kilometers long.

On the north, Afghanistan is bounded by the USSR. The 350-kilometer border lies primarily along the Amu-Darya River. In the west it borders Iran (820 kilometers); in the south and east it borders Pakistan and northern Kashmir (2,180 kilometers); in the northeast it touches China along the Hindu Kush (75 kilometers).

The country does not have any access to the sea. The closest water is the Persian Gulf, some 500 kilometers to the southwest. Mountains make up nearly 80 percent of the territory, with peaks more than 7 kilometers high.

The population is scattered in this mountainous area. According to the only general census, held in June 1979, the Afghan population is about 15.5 million people, including more than twenty nationalities. The majority of Afghans are Pushtun, some 9.5 million people. The Tadzhiks are the second largest group, with more than 3 million people. There are Uzbeks, Turkomen, Kirghiz, Nuristanis, Kazakhs, Baluch,

151

and Arabs. About 90 percent of the population from age fifteen to sixty can neither read nor write; 99 percent of women are illiterate. Ethnic minorities are practically 100 percent illiterate, for they usually do not have written languages. People speak mainly Pushtu and Dari.

Throughout the history of Afghanistan the Pushtuns have had a privileged position. More than once this has triggered national disturbances and conflicts. The new Afghan government that came to power in April 1978 made public its intention to do away with all forms of racial, language, and ethnic discrimination.

The Pushtun population is still divided into tribes. The Durrani (more than 1.5 million) is the largest, followed by Gilzai (under 1.5 million), the Kurraki (500,000), and the smaller Huriakel and Ysufzai. The tribes populate the south, southeast, and some northern parts of Afghanistan.

The Durrani tribe is the most influential. All the emirs starting with Dost Muhammed (1826–1863), the kings, and President M. Daud came from this tribe.

The Tadzhiks live mostly in the north and central parts of the country. They are influential in both agricultural areas and the cities.

The Uzbeks live in the northern and some central parts of Afghanistan, with agriculture and cattle-raising their main occupations. In the mountain areas they lead a seminomad life-style.

The Hazara speak one of the dialects of the Tadzhik language. They populate the mountainous area of central Afghanistan situated between Kabul and Herat. This region is called Hazarajat. The Hazaras are settled people. They are famous as consummate masters of irrigation works in mountain areas.

The Turkomen live in the northern regions bordering on the USSR. Their major occupation is nomad and seminomad cattle-raising. Some Turkomen cultivate the land but they are few.

The Nuristani populate northeastern Afghanistan. It is a mountainous area in the Hindu Kush. The Moslem population of the country used to call the nationality by the scornful name *kafir* ("faithless") because the people persisted in retaining their ancient religious traditions. Even the region where the Nuristani lived has been called Kafiristan, "the land of the faithless."

The overwhelming majority of the Afghan population is Moslem, professing Islam. Having emerged in western Arabia the religion spread to Afghanistan at the end of the seventh and the beginning of the eighth centuries. Islam did not convert the entire population of the country at once; the process was actually rather slow. In Kabul, for example, Islam became firmly established no earlier than the end of the ninth century. Before Islam, the population of Kabul professed Buddhism.

Appendix B

DOCUMENTATION AND RESEARCH

_____

The approach of Soviet scientists to the Afghans in the first postrevolution years (after October 1917) was guided by their desire to closely link the victory of the socialist revolution in Russia and the upheaval of the national-liberation struggle in Afghanistan. They also tried to emphasize that the Russian revolution had created auspicious conditions for the successful outcome of the Afghan struggle that was fiercely opposed by international and Afghan reactionary forces.

The first accounts of Soviet-Afghan relations came out soon after the restoration of Afghan independence in 1919 in the pages of the magazines *Zhizn Nastionalnostey* ("Life of Nationalities"), an organ of the People's Commissariat on Nationalities, *Novi y Vostok* ("New East"), an organ of the Oriental Studies Scientific Association attached to the People's Commissariat on Nationalities, and the *Voennaya Mysl* ("Military Thought"), published by the Revolutionary Military Council of the Turkestan Front in Tashkent. These articles were of keen political character, pointedly critical of the British policy in Afghanistan.

A distinguished Soviet diplomat and statesman, G. V. Chicherin, in his 1961 book *Articles and Speeches on Foreign Policy Issues* came to this conclusion: "Despite certain difficulties, we have had in Afghanistan a friend and an ally, and we are convinced that our friendly relations do have a future."

Chicherin's statements on the Soviet foreign policy buildup testify to the importance the Soviet Union gave to friendship with its southern neighbor. In his article in 1962, "Mysteries of the International Situation," Chicherin pointed out: "It is clear to any observer that the cause of Afghan revival and Afghan independence succeeded because independent and reviving Afghanistan can fully rely on the friendship of its northern neighbor." Chicherin convincingly described the mutually advantageous character of Soviet-Afghan relations. At the same time his article "A Year of Soviet Oriental Policy" demonstrated how difficult and tense the struggle around the 1921 Soviet-Afghan treaty in Afghanistan was.

Of great interest is the book *The USSR Foreign Policy: Speeches and Statements (1927–1935)* by People's Commissar on Foreign Affairs M. M. Litvinov, published in 1935. It contains valuable information on Soviet relations with other countries. Litvinov claims that the Soviet Union regarded Afghanistan as a fully sovereign, independent state and never interfered in its home affairs regardless of what was going on in Afghan society, or whether the Soviet government liked it or not. Touching upon the developments of 1929, a most dramatic period of Afghan history, when power passed from one faction to another, Litvinov noted: "Afghanistan was going through tumult, which, of course, caused our concern, for we sincerely want its people to retain independence."

The first Soviet summary works on Afghanistan emerged in the second part of the 1920s. This research was focused on the state of Soviet-Afghan relations and their history. Political evaluations were based on the official documents of that time, namely as the People's Commissariat on Foreign Affairs prepared reports to the Congress of the Soviets.

An outstanding scientist-orientalist, Professor Ivan Reisner (1899–1958), was the founder of Afghan studies in the USSR. After diplomatic relations between Soviet Russia and Afghanistan had been established, he worked in the Soviet mission in Kabul for two years. Reisner's works on Afghanistan are still significant; they help us to understand better the socioeconomic trends of development not only in Afghanistan but in the East as a whole.

Although the historic aspect of Soviet-Afghan relations was not a subject of Reisner's specific research, his books *Independent Afghanistan,*

Afghanistan, and A Decade of Afghan Foreign Policy show the Soviet role in restoring Afghan independence and Soviet assistance in the social and economic development of Afghanistan.

Reisner urged the Soviet government to maintain a consistent course aimed at strengthening its friendship with Afghanistan between 1919 and 1928, despite certain negative actions, such as Afghan support for the basmach (Moslem guerrilla) robber bands in Soviet Central Asia. Pressure was exerted on Amanullah Khan and his associates by Afghan forces to make him support the *basmachi*.

In the years immediately preceding World War II, there was little historic research on Soviet-Afghan relations. In postwar years, works by R. T. Akhramovich on Soviet-Afghan relations between 1961 and 1966 were published. The author analyzed Soviet-Afghan relations from the viewpoint of peaceful coexistence of states with different social systems, leaving out the then fashionable Soviet principle of proletariat internationalism.

In the late 1950s and early 1960s, the role of national bourgeoisie in the Oriental countries, including Afghanistan, came to the attention of historians. This used to draw vigorous criticism, since the national bourgeoisie was viewed as the enemy of the working people.

The new stage in Afghan studies was developed over the next decade, connected with social, political, economic, and cultural changes in Afghanistan. This was important for the developments of April 1978, primarily their military aspects. Research of Soviet-Afghan economic cooperation was carried out by N. M. Gurevich[1] and can be singled out among others. Ample data illustrates the importance for Afghanistan of its trade and economic links with the Soviet Union, particularly in terms of strengthening its economic independence. Gurevich held that the incentive of Afghan leadership to cooperate economically with the USSR was determined by both political and true economic reasons.

Y. M. Golovin wrote a book and a series of articles describing the experience of Soviet-Afghan economic cooperation.[2] Soviet-Afghan economic links, in his opinion, allow Afghanistan to strengthen its standing in world markets and the international arena. Golovin showed that even prowestern sections in Afghanistan had to concede that the wide-ranging trade and economic cooperation with the Soviet Union were beneficial to Afghanistan.

Research in the history of Soviet-Afghan relations at large, carried out by Soviet writers, reflects the official attitude of the Soviet leadership toward these relations. It boils down to the thesis that the Soviet drive to develop friendly ties with Afghanistan is a principled policy. This explains the fact that the Soviet Union had been promoting friendship and cooperation with the neighboring country since October 1917. Another theme running through these studies of Soviet-Afghan relations is that Soviet policy toward Afghanistan is to the advantage of that country and its people and whatever the USSR is doing is in the best interests of the Afghan people.

At the same time, students from other countries described Soviet-Afghan relations differently.

Afghan postgraduates who studied abroad, particularly those who received their education in the USSR, wrote a number of dissertations on Soviet-Afghan relations. The research by A. K. Kushi, "Development of Afghan-Soviet Relations (1946–1969)," is written by a supporter of good-neighboring relations between the two countries. Despite being fully in tune with the official foreign policy position of the ruling dynasty, the author insisted on an "equal approach" to both the USSR and western countries by Afghanistan. The main idea of these writings contradicted most Soviet works in this field which always emphasized that Afghanistan should give its relations with the USSR top priority.

M. A. Mehra's dissertation, "The Afghan Policy of Neutrality and Nonalignment," posited that the Afghan policy of neutrality and non-alignment with any superpower blocs gives Afghanistan worldwide authority and is the main reason for the good attitude of other countries, including the USSR.

In 1970 an Afghan scientist, N. Tarsi, defended his doctoral dissertation in The University of Paris. His research was on Soviet-Afghan relations. Paying tribute to the Soviet role in Afghan economic development and buildup, he stressed the importance of western aid, including Great Britain's. He tried to prove that Afghanistan was a key model for Third World countries; while retaining its independence and neutrality, a country could enjoy assistance from the superpowers.

Works by western authors are rather remarkable too, differing greatly from those by both Soviet and Afghan authors. Some of them doubt the sincerity of Soviet-Afghan relations, while the role of western countries and their policies toward Afghanistan are shown in a different light.

Afghan studies by western writers can be divided into three chronological periods.

1. In the years before and after World War II, the main aim of western studies was to show Soviet attempts to bend Afghanistan to its will along with establishing diplomatic relations with her southern neighbor. The USSR viewed it as the first step in its strategic desire to approach the Indian Ocean.

The 1940 two-volume *History of Afghanistan* by British writer P. Sykes is the most extensive research published at that time in the West. Its annotation reads that it is the "first and complete history of Afghanistan." The author's purpose was to "provide British official circles and the public at large with true information about the country." In terms of foreign policy aspects of Afghan history, Sykes's main aim was to prove that the Soviet Union, like tzarist Russia in the past, was an everlasting threat to Afghanistan, whereas Great Britain had been and would always remain a guarantor of its independence. The author claims that the restoration of Afghan independence came as a result of faultless British policy rather than the struggle of the Afghan people and Soviet support for the struggle as Soviet authors stated it.

We mention Sykes's research because many western scientists used it as a basis for their own approach to Soviet-Afghan relations. This is true for prominent British diplomat W. K. Fraser-Tytler, the author of the well-known book *Afghanistan: A Study of Political Developments in Central Asia* (London, 1959). The author described Soviet intentions in Afghanistan as aggressive. Like Sykes, he gave priority to the British policy in Afghanistan.

2. From the second half of the 1950s until the 1978 April revolution, western students concentrated their attention on Soviet-Afghan economic cooperation.

One of the most notable authors in that period is Vartan Gregorian. A Lebanese by origin, he worked at Stanford University in California and became famous for his book *The Emergence of Modern Afghanistan: The Policy of Reform and Modernization, 1880–1946*. Based on numerous sources, including those from the Soviet Union, his work contains a series of theses in which the author admits the difference between policies of the USSR and tzarist Russia. His viewpoint is that when the victory of the October revolution wiped away the threat of aggression from the north, Afghanistan no longer thought it urgent to remain in the orbit of British influence.

It is characteristic of western researchers that they failed to realize that it was not easy for Soviet Russia to provide economic aid to Afghanistan in the first postrevolution years. Pointing out that there was practically no aid at all, western authors would not admit that the country itself was going through a most difficult time, and in fact was itself facing all kinds of shortages.

One of the first in the history of international relations, the Soviet-Afghan treaty, dated February 28, 1921, got a peculiar interpretation. American author G. Spector in his book *The Soviet Union and the Moslem World, 1917–1958* qualifies the document as an incarnation of insidious plans on both sides: It allowed Afghanistan to secure the emirate regime in Bukhara and the khanate in Khiva, and allowed Soviet Russia to create a "key" anti-British and anti-Indian "propaganda center."

Some western researchers regard Afghanistan as a field for competition between East and West. A group of authors, with L. Dupree and L. Albert as editors, in 1974 published in New York an anthology in which Soviet-British rivalry in Afghanistan is described. The authors write that even after 1919, Afghanistan remained a zone of British and Soviet interests and that both countries tried to benefit from their relations with Afghanistan. At the same time an American economist, Peter Frank, considers that the U.S. policy in Afghanistan is the same as the Russian's.

If historic statements are accurate, the peak of Soviet-Afghan economic cooperation was during 1955–1973, when the Soviet Union after Stalin's death threw off the fetters of the personality cult and could develop trade with other countries. It was the period when the Soviet Union built a series of important industrial and agricultural enterprises in Afghanistan. Nevertheless, many western writers fail to mention these facts. An American professor, Charles B. MacLean, for example, worked in the Soviet Union for a long time and was well aware of Soviet-Afghan relations. In his book *"Soviet-Asian Relations,"* published in London in 1973, while stressing the significance of Soviet-Afghan economic links, he leaves out various facts and data, thus depriving his book of convincing information.

But Professor G. Etienne of the International Research University and the Africa Institute in Geneva, unambiguously claims that the Soviet Union, although meeting the Afghan request to render assistance in the construction of a huge irrigation system in the Jalalabad region, was guided by political rather than economic priorities. Etienne contends that the desire to strengthen its positions south of the Hindu Kush close to Pakistan caused the Soviet Union to assume this responsibility.[3]

H. Byroade, a former U.S. ambassador in Kabul, is of the same opinion. He thinks that the Soviet Union chose Afghanistan as a battlefield to wage its "economic cold war."[4] American writer H. Armstrong sounds convincing in his opinion on Soviet-Afghan relations: "Giving Afghanistan economic help, the USSR was guided by a quite natural longing to draw Afghanistan to its orbit."[5] The American C. Sulzberger wrote, "Can a poverty-stricken country repay its debts and have anything to export to other countries?"[6]

There is a marked tendency in western works on the one hand to disregard Soviet economic aid to Afghanistan or depreciate its role, while on the other hand holding the USSR responsible for Afghan economic backwardness. An American writer, R. King, considers the effect of Soviet aid as "surprisingly insignificant."[7] Professor G. Etienne blames the USSR for Afghan financial and economic troubles.

3. After the 1978 April revolution, a number of books about Afghanistan were published in which the authors estimated negatively the developments in the country as well as Soviet-Afghan relations. They accused the Soviet Union of preparations to overthrow the Afghan regime and to interfere in the internal affairs of a sovereign state. L. E. Nicksh (United States); Faiz-ur-Rahman, Bashir A. Khureishi, Saied Shabbir Hussein, A. N. Alvi, and A. N. Risvi (all Pakistan) were among the authors who wrote on the subject. Professor Beverly Male of the Australian Royal Military College wrote that H. Amin fell victim in the struggle against Soviet attempts to draw Afghanistan into the sphere of Soviet influence.[8]

However, there are western researchers who have an opposite point of view. A history professor at the University in Delhi, A. Ansari, in his book of collected articles *Developments in Afghanistan through Indian Eyes* (Delhi, 1980), pays tribute to Amanullah Khan, who strove to develop friendly relations with the Soviet Union, as he emphasizes the importance of the Soviet-Afghan 1921 treaty. He does not share some of his western colleagues' opinion that the activities of USSR and Afghan revolutionary forces triggered the arms race and worsened the situation.

The years after the April revolution, the civil war, and Soviet military interference provided information for politicians, economists, and researchers to have a more realistic look at Soviet-Afghan relations with all historic developments considered. The nine-year military involvement of Soviet troops in the Afghan war needs a thorough analysis of the reasons, aims, and, most importantly, the aftermath of the act. The course of combat action itself, its analysis, a comparison of the arms and combat equipment of the warring sides, and worldwide reaction to the war are addressed in this book.

NOTES

1. N. M. Gurevich, *Economic Development of Afghanistan*, 1967.
2. Y. M. Golovin, *The Soviet Union and Afghanistan,* 1962.
3. G. L. Etienne, *Afghanistan en Voie de Collaboration,* 1972, 203.
4. H. Byroade, *Changing Position of Afghanistan, Washington in Asia,* (Washington: 1961) 10.
5. H. Armstrong, "North of the Khyber," *Foreign Affairs,* Vol. 34, No. 4 (1956): 604.
6. C. Sulzberger, *The Unfinished Revolution: America and the Third World* (N.Y.: 1965), 185–186.
7. R. King, *Afghanistan: Cockpit in High Asia* (N.Y.: 1966), 57.
8. Beverly Male, *Revolutionary Afghanistan: A Reappraisal* (Canberra, 1982).

Appendix C

War's Impact on Soldiers and Families

One of Many

Yura is one of those who has been hurt by the Afghan war. He does not trust anybody. And although he has not seen war for a single day, his faith in people has been killed by the war.

Yura is twenty-four, skinny and awkward, and a Siberian. His father is a driller; his mother is an accountant. He learned radio mechanics. He did not shirk service in the army, but came into collision with "orders" in the army the very first day, when he received an order to change his civilian clothes for a uniform. The warrant officer whipped those who lagged behind with a belt. After training, he joined the echelon to Tashkent. There he learned that they were being sent to "defend the southern frontiers of our Motherland." He did not think over those words much. If we are threatened, he reasoned, it is necessary to defend the country.

In Kabul he was more threatened by the "old men."* On the seventh day of his stay in Afghanistan, not waiting for the next "inves-

----

*"Old men" are soldiers in the last year of their military service; those who, as a rule, scoff at the young soldiers, make them do their work, and beat them unmercifully.

tigation," he climbed over the barbed wire and started running. It seemed to him that to reach the next unit was child's play. But nothing came of it. He was stopped by some people in turbans.

He escaped from them in ten days, when the Mujahidin, accustomed to his humility, relaxed their attention. He hid in the mountains. The ragged shoes that were given to him instead of boots became frozen, and his legs were covered with hoarfrost. He started back to his own forces, swallowing tears of pain, offense, and fright. He almost succeeded; he could already see the lights of Kabul. But again he ran into rebel soldiers. They introduced themselves as the people's militia; they promised to help. They "helped."

They brought him to Pakistan on a donkey, since he could not walk. He was thrown down in a courtyard; he was kicked several times. One asked how many "fighters for faith" he had killed. He replied that he had just arrived. How the western journalists heard about him he does not know even now. But in the end, with the help of the International Red Cross, on January 14, 1983, he found himself in Switzerland.

In 1980 the first news about the Soviet soldiers taken prisoner in Afghanistan reached the USSR. The nondeclared war was carefully concealed at that time. On their tombstones, they wrote simply "dead." There was a ban even to call soldiers prisoners of war. They would say "fallen into the hands of bandits."

But the Ministry of Foreign Affairs and the Ministry of Defense of the USSR and the Soviet Committee of the Red Cross appealed to various international organizations for help. In two years agreements were reached with the International Committee of the Red Cross. Its representatives promised to provide assistance in rescuing Soviet soldiers from captivity and transferring them to Switzerland, to the Zougerberg camp. They established one primary condition: The term of incarceration in the camp was two years. After that a man would have the right to choose. If he desired, he could return to the USSR; if not, he could stay in the West. This latter condition was not popular in Moscow.

Some eleven persons were processed through Switzerland.

Yura later told this story:

We were approximately in the same position as Swiss soldiers under punishment. We looked after cows, fed hens, and mowed the grass. They treated my legs and employed me on easy work. I washed dishes. Nobody urged us on; we worked as we could.

We received 240 francs per month. On days off, we made excursions to the nearby town. In short, during that half year, I was treated as a man for the first time. And as for going home, I was afraid to do it. I knew how they had treated the captives in 1945. And if I would not go home, why drag on for two years in camp? Once when we came to the town, I dropped behind and caught a taxi. I finally reached Germany and asked for political asylum.

One can imagine the reaction that was caused among Soviet military men and diplomats when they learned of Yura's flight. It was only the first straw. The second one broke the camel's back. When another two men from Switzerland did not want to go back to Russia, the decision was made to decline the assistance of the International Committee of the Red Cross in the future.

Yura did not complain of his life in Germany. If the dole was not sufficient, he was able to earn additional money. He learned the language and rented an apartment. In the meantime in the USSR perestroika was announced. Within three years the procurator general announced amnesty for the captives. Having not clearly decided whether he could go home, he dropped in at the Soviet consulate.

In a day he was in the Soviet Union, where only several months before he would have been given ten to fifteen years in prison for all these adventures.

Here in short is a story of one of those who, if fortune had not smiled upon him, could have been reported missing. And upon how many men of his age has fortune not smiled?

Living on "Hope"

According to official statistics, during the war in Afghanistan 330 Soviet persons were missing. But this is according to the official statistics.

From the card file of the People's Committee for Release of the Soviet Prisoners of War, "Hope":

No. 30, Lisniak, Nickolai Vasilievitch, born in 1964. Called up in September 1982. Sent to the Kandahar landing and assault battalion. On December 29, 1982, he reported for duty. He did not return to his unit. His parents insisted on opening his coffin; inside there was another man.

No. 155, Arbouzov, Pavel Dmitrievitch. Born in 1936. Civilian. Was sent on a mission by the Ministry of the Gas Industry of the USSR to Shibirghan. Along with two Afghans, he went for food. On their way back they were taken prisoner. A death certificate was issued.

No. 168, Novikov, Igor Evgenievitch. Called up on October 1, 1983. Served in Jalalabad. Was reported missing on January 23, 1984. According to eyewitness accounts, he was sent to bring wood but did not come back. Searches found signs of a fight, a torn belt.

There are 415 cards in the card index of "Hope."

It is possible that Yura's story is not the most typical one. But how is one to determine the most typical? Someone was not found after a battle; someone was hit in an ambush; some did not come back upon having gone to a village for purchases. There were some who were taken prisoner by their own carelessness, and for lack of experience. There are some who left of their own will, for reasons known only to them.

For nine years of the war only about fifty men have been freed. Out of them, thirty-one have returned to the USSR; the rest are in the West. According to the International Committee for the Release of the Soviet Prisoners of War, about seventy-five men survived in Afghanistan and Pakistan.

Were you or your nearest relatives in captivity or in internment during the Great Patriotic War? Where, when, and under what circumstances were they released? These queries are contained in some questionnaires. In them are the attitudes of Soviet official organs toward prisoners of war: watchful, distrustful, deliberately assuming some guilt in a man without any reason. And does one wonder that during the Afghan war the problem of prisoners of war was in the background? Of course, one can find sufficient convincing explanations of that if one wishes. There is no mention of it in the Geneva accord. But it was necessary to settle more important, strategic questions. The Soviets did not think of it during the withdrawal of the troops. But they were faced with the task of bringing home tens of thousands, and there were only a few, not even a hundred who were missing. They have rescued only a few men. They said that the opposition was intractable.

Maybe. But how to consider this fact, then? A principal of the organization Freedom House, an American, Liudmila Thorn, for three years has literally pulled out by hand fifteen men from Pakistan, almost one-third of those released. An American woman, alone. She succeeded by herself in having a meeting with President Reagan; she went to the leaders of the "seven"; she by herself made the rounds of the camps of the Mujahidin. Our giants with their great resources, extensive contacts, and a net of representatives all over the world could not do it.

Several years ago in the United States there was founded the International Committee for the Release of the Soviet Prisoners of War in Afghanistan. It was headed by the painter Michael Shemiakin. Soviet journalist Iona Andronov became a member of the committee. However, he did not come to terms with the Americans and soon after he was excluded. Who is to blame? But that's not the point. One thing is known: Those who are in captivity did not gain from the scandal. In 1988, a similar Soviet committee was founded. Better late than never; the only thing that counts is results. And there are still none of them. The list of those who are united in the committee and those who became its members will take up a good half page of the newspaper sheet, from the Committee of the Youth Organizations of the USSR to the Committee of the Veterans of the War, from a singer to an expert of the Central Council of Trade Unions. Letters are written and unconsoling replies are received. Negotiations are held and statements in sympathy with our sorrow are accepted.

It was not because of a comfortable life that in February 1991, mothers of the missing and interested persons united in the people's committee, "Hope." They took on themselves what the state should have done: help widows and mothers, search for eyewitnesses of death or the capture of soldiers, care for those who came back. There are many letters such as the following in "Hope" files.

> . . . mother of Misha Iashkov is writing to you. He has not come back from Afghanistan. I have been waiting for him for many years. Maybe my son is in captivity. How many tears have been shed for all those years, how many sleepless nights? I have lost my son in a foreign land. Why? I buried my husband and was left alone. I am 64 years old. I have been waiting for my son and I shall wait for him until my last days. . . .

One has often heard that the people will not understand the general amnesty. One ought not to say so for everybody. The officer who drove a father of a missing son to distraction by having called his son a traitor considered himself one of "the people." And those who hunted down the parents, brokenhearted enough anyway, and forced them to move to another town, are they not also "people?"

We did not identify Yura, whose story was told in the beginning, by his surname. We have recently learned that he did not remain over here. He went back, forever. And a Soviet journalist has already written that Yura would not shake hands with him. It seems to us that that is the simplest thing to do.

Russian military leaders have said that a war ends when the last captive is released. About seventy-five Soviet soldiers are now in captivity.

Changing Attitudes

What was expected of those who came back after the war, having gone down its fiery roads?

A newspaper of the army was kind enough to give us a number of letters of the "Afgantsi," in which they describe the soul of those men who have been hurt in the war, how much they have seen and experienced in Afghanistan, and how they have been moving about for months and years, not finding the support and understanding of their associates.

> Hello, dear editorial staff! One of the men who are now called the "Afgantsi" is writing to you. I have read your article dated the 21st of December, "Afghanistan is aching in my soul," and decided to write to you. I served in Afghanistan in 1983–1985. Everything was there during that time: battle outposts, alarms in the middle of the night, and going on operations. I watched as my close friends were killed, those with whom I had spoken only ten to twenty minutes before. I came back from Afghanistan in August 1985. I did not know what to do or where to go. I did not find understanding among my friends and all my family. My nerves started to fail. I decided to leave my native village for some place as far away as possible. My mother died in 1984 when I was serving in the forces, but they did not even allow me to go to her funeral. I am working now at a cotton-spinning factory in Ivanteevka. Here are other lads, "Afgantsi" too. And I am happy that if only among them I can find understanding. A. Zavoronkov.

The family of disabled soldier-internationalist A. S. Rymartchuk from the city of Kursk, has communicated with the Ministry of Social Security of the Tadzhik SSR. Rymartchuk came back from Afghanistan without a leg. From 1984 to 1987 he was granted the second order of disablement, but in November 1988 he was moved to the third order of disablement. This means that his pension will be reduced considerably to about fifty rubles and he will lose a number of other privileges. His forms are stamped as follows: "in accordance with the instructions," and "not possible."

Much to our regret, pensions of invalids are lagging far behind increasing prices. Many men who returned from Afghanistan as invalids cannot survive without material help from their parents. And they are young. Their life is ahead of them. How will this turn out?

Another letter:

Some time ago I met with soldier-internationalists in medical rehabilitation center *Rus'* ("Russia") in the town of Rouza near Moscow. Schoolchildren have earned money and have purchased some apples from a state farm. I brought the apples to the hospital. I cannot describe how moved the soldier-"Afgantsi" were. A month and a half has passed since I returned, but I have not yet been able to recover from the experience. I believe that I shall not forget it as long as I live. I really pity the lads who were crippled in Afghanistan. They have so many problems that are settled so slowly by the organizations concerned. One cannot even imagine that such things can happen in our country. One of the men told me that for six years he had exhausted his family's means. Every year he must stay in the hospital for three to four months, because his pension is so small. It has turned out that what the family earned for the last year is being spent on him. Many of the men do not have any specialized training.

It is necessary that the entire country should understand the privations and unsettled state of these men. It is necessary to report about them on television more often and to write about them in the newspapers. They deserve it. We must ensure that the "Afgantsi" do not lose faith in us and are not afraid of their future. G. Gelvikh, Bondarevka village, Markovsky district, Voroshilovgradsky region.

Another letter reminds us of the guilt of the society as it relates to the Afgantsi. The word *charity* is like "pie in the sky" nowadays. Having discovered it, we are using the term much more often, experiencing a wordy euphoria, using it as a password. In short, we are not down to earth. The truth is that our everyday help is so very small for those who need it. It seems that their descendants will see with surprise films filled with endless parades, fashion shows, and charitable events and slogans left from our days. They may be surprised by how little truth there is among those dazzling tales we used to tell about the men who came back from Afghanistan, about their troubles and hopes, about those who were crippled at twenty. Our charity resides in the past and in the future. What about the present?

Medals on the breast of an "Afgan"—what stands behind each of them? A battle in a gorge surrounded by the Mujahidin? A rush under fire to a comrade bleeding to death? A rescue of wounded from a vehicle on fire? All that was in that war. And every decoration was won in a battle. One would think, could it be possible to encounter indifference in such sacred deeds as the presentation of a decoration? It appears that it is possible.

Hello, editorial staff. I have never written to newspapers, but now I have decided to do it. The problem is that during my service in Afghanistan I was recommended for the Order of the Red Star. But I have not been presented with it, although a copy of the certificate of the medal is in my personal file with a reference number, complete with all signatures and stamps. More than two years have passed since the time of my recommendation for the decoration, but no presentation. V. Ostrovsky, st. Mirnaya, Tchitinsky region.

Says Ilia Golubev from the town of Berdiansk of the Zaporozsky region to the editors:

I need the truth. In 1986 for an operation in the region of Herat I was recommended for the Medal for Bravery. More than two years have passed since that time, but the medal has not been presented to me. If the headquarters have deprived me of that decoration, please inform me, for what reason exactly. That decoration is very precious to me, and I think it is not necessary to explain why.

How strangely and cruelly the courage shown in battle, and some clerk's indifference or sluggishness became evident in that correspondence.

The editorial staff has sent copies of those letters to the Ministry of Defense of the USSR and requested them to conclude a competent review of every complaint connected with a recommended decoration.

Many other letters are about our overall lack of housing. Many sick and wounded "Afgan" soldiers, having left the hospitals, now are finding themselves homeless.

Dear editorial staff! Here are "Afgan" soldiers from the city of Ivanovo writing to you. Our friend Alexander Gousev already has been working for three years as a driver at the motor-crane factory in our city. He is married and they are awaiting a child. Before the wedding, Alexander lived in the factory's hostel, where he is registered. Before the ceremony, his wife lived in the hostel of the factory where she works and where she is also registered. This young Gousev family has rented a room for which they pay 30 rubles. The house managers have not registered the Gousevs with them, so they are paying also for the hostels. The latest blow is that the hostel manager was categorically ordered to remove them from the list of tenants. And this is just before the birth of a child when it is even more necessary to support the family. How and where can they live? Where to apply? Alexander has visited many offices, but all in vain. Is it possible that Alexander Gousev, marked with traces of the Afghan's bullets, who had to lie in a hospital for almost a year, does not deserve at least one room for him and his family?

In the so-called stagnant years, many useful policies were adopted that seem to hang in midair. Therefore, in the time of glasnost, it is important to know what extra subsidies are allocated to provide housing for the Afgantsi. The fact that various policies have been adopted about privileges for the "Afgans" in itself does not increase the number of flats.

Here are statistics cited by A. Zavoronkov from Ivanteevka, whose letter we have already quoted.

I have a wife and two children. But when we shall live in our own flat we do not know. I am on a preferential waiting list established by the town executive committee. My ordinal number is 203, and on the general waiting list it is 1,115. As for joining a cooperative, it is more than I, as well as my "Afgan" friends, can afford. Why is it so difficult to obtain what is a basic right?

It is understandable that in the letters and responses, Armenia and Afghanistan are put side by side. With regard to the scope of the tragedy and to the circles of misfortune, such are spreading on earth. By their consequences, events in Afghanistan are on the same order with the Armenian earthquake. In its way, tremors make themselves felt in all towns and villages. The opinion of the people can be learned from the following lines:

> Your newspaper has raised the question of the inadequate pensions of invalids. I would like to know what pensions are granted in other countries for persons who lose their health in the army. I believe that our aid to invalids should be at least 200 rubles per month, although even that is not at all sufficient for those who were crippled in battle. The same pension should also be paid to mothers who have lost their children. One might say, "where will the state find such money?" Let us all work several extra days a year to help the invalids of the war. No honest person will refuse to do it. A. A. Veber, Tomsk.

Writes I. Matveev, a former soldier and father of three sons from the Bolshoi Kamen village of the Primorsk region:

> This is the last straw, that in our country, after this war, cripples are appearing in markets with outstretched hands: "Please give alms for bread to a soldier-internationalist." It's a scandal known all over the world! Let us not allow it!

It is also because of anxiety for the fate of "Afgan" soldiers that T. Liakovskaia wrote:

> For a long ten years we have waited for that day—the 15th of February 1989. Thanks to perestroika, it has come. Let it be the day of memory for everyone who perished in that dreadful and long war.

*   *   *

Many other writers suggest that a long-term state program of aid to soldier-internationalists should be worked out. They have earned it.

EFFECTS ON THE ARMED FORCES

The consequences of the Afghan war have tended to corrupt the entire state of the armed forces. According to estimates of investigators, the scale of military crimes, desertion, and loss of servicemen had increased.

About 4.5 million persons today are serving in the armed forces. Annually, almost 7,000 servicemen die during peacetime conditions. This is a large number for a nonaggressive country, almost 1.5 deaths per thousand, about 50 percent higher than one death per thousand in similar conditions in the U.S. Army.

The Ministry of Defense of the USSR alleges that the majority of these men perish through their own fault, suicide, negligence, and accidents. However, thousands of parents of these soldiers believe that their sons were killed through some official negligence or murder and that the officials, not wishing to disclose information on crimes in their ranks, are trying to conceal the truth.

A Soviet officer having access to the statistics of the Ministry of Defense has informed us that "many more soldiers die under mysterious circumstances than the military recognizes even in the reports destined for official use."

These official confidential statistics show that 18 percent of such deaths are suicides, 5.5 percent are the result of crimes, 13.5 percent as a result of accidents, 17 percent from not observing industrial safety, 21 percent from disease, 15 percent from road accidents, and 9.5 percent from careless handling of firearms.

Our informant said that from other ministerial documents it is clear that even in secret information the statistics are falsified. "Many murders are concealed in such categories as accidents, diseases, and misuse of some machinery. Even in military commands, it would be too dangerous to disclose the truth. I think that this is one of the most morbid and terrible secrets of the Soviet Army."

Families of deceased soldiers consider that the "concealed murders" constitute the overwhelming majority. They spend their time in search of justice, but cannot find peace even at night. They openly demand investigations into the deaths of their sons. For many years these demands have been ignored, until they established the Committee of Soldiers' Mothers.

Under its pressure, President Mikhail Gorbachev in November 1990 set up a special consulting commission to investigate these accusations. It has already recommended to civil authorities that they conduct recurring investigations of thousands of cases, but, the commission does not have the authority to order them to perform as recommended.

These accusations, that the military leaders have concealed systematically murders of soldiers, appear at a time when the army is subject to growing criticism in other areas.

The people protest the use of the army for suppression of people's rights. Servicemen are returning from Eastern Europe to depressed living conditions. The youth, especially in the regions involved in nationalistic disturbances, ignore conscription orders, and the desertion rate has lately reached record figures.

Apart from those who refuse to serve, up to 20 percent of conscripts "do not meet physical and mental norms," declared Col. Valery Volin, secretary of the commission. He believes that these factors are the main reason for the suspicious deaths and agrees with growing demands for setting up an army entirely on a voluntary basis.

Not all the cases under investigation are murders or crimes, said Elena Varenko, a military lawyer working in the commission: "It is difficult for parents to recognize it, but sometimes their son, whom they thought mentally normal, nevertheless decides to commit suicide or meets with an accident." Despite this, she thinks that the military investigators "heap up so many lies that the truth itself looks dubious."

THE OFFICIAL CONDEMNATION

The Afghan Syndrome has also manifested itself in an official condemnation by the Soviet Union on participation of the Soviet armed forces in the war in Afghanistan. On October 25, 1989, the Supreme Soviet of the USSR made a sharp political assessment on the decision of intervention in Afghanistan. They emphasized that this decision deserved both moral and political condemnation. Their document stated that the general international situation in which the decision was made was, of course, complicated, characterized by a difficult political confrontation. There were notions of intentions of some circles in the United States to take revenge in Afghanistan for the loss of position that happened after the fall of the shah's regime in Iran. Such was possible.

The paper stated that one of the motives for the actions taken was the desire to strengthen the security of the Soviet Union on the approaches to her southern frontiers, considering the tension that was present in Afghanistan at that time. There were increasing signs of armed outside interference. There were appeals of the Afghan government to the Soviet leadership for aid, to include military units.

The decision of December 1979 was, of course, influenced by excessive ideological guidelines dealing with Soviet foreign economic activity, which had been formed for many years. The government stated that one question dealt with a limited task—assistance in protecting communications and various individual projects. However, all those circumstances cannot justify the decision to intervene with troops in Afghanistan.

How did the situation develop, in reality, later on? The extent of clashes became longer and harder. The Soviet armed forces contingent became involved in large-scale military actions. International tension, mistrust, and military and political competition between the East and West were aggravated.

The prestige of Soviet policy among a considerable part of the international community declined. By this action the USSR became opposed to the majority of the world community and norms of behavior that have been adopted and observed in international intercourse.

The intervention decision was made in defiance of the Constitution of the USSR (clause 73, paragraph 8) in accord with which, "questions of peace and war, defense of the country's sovereignty, defense of the frontiers and territories of the USSR, organization of defense, direction of the armed forces of the USSR" are under the jurisdiction of the Union of the Soviet Socialist Republics in the person of its supreme bodies of state power and administration.

The Supreme Soviet of the USSR and its Presidium did not have a chance to consider the question of sending the troops to Afghanistan. The decision was made by a narrow circle of persons. The Politburo of the Communist party did not even bring its complete membership together to discuss the question and to approve the decision.

The names of those who made the decision are: Leonid Brezhnev, occupying at that time the posts of the general secretary of the CC of the CPSU, chairman of the Presidium of the Supreme Soviet of the country, chairman of the Council of Defense, and the supreme commander of the armed forces of the USSR; former minister of defense of the USSR, Dmitry Ustinov; the chairman of the Committee of the State Security of the USSR (KGB), Yuri Andropov; and the minister of foreign affairs of the USSR, Andrei Gromyko.

The decision for such an important action, bypassing the supreme bodies of state power of the country, without any participation by the people, became possible because of serious flaws in the system of formulating practical policy and the ultimate mechanism of making decisions. In accord with the practice established at that time, this decision should have been submitted for discussion by some political or public forum. Had that happened, the policy would have most likely been approved. But, as it was, the party, the people, and foreign friends of the USSR were confronted with a fait accompli.

Today, policy based on new thinking would eliminate the possibility of a repetition of anything like the action of 1979. There is now real control in the supreme bodies of the administration over the process of formation and execution of foreign policy by the newly independent republics. Foreign policy must always be controlled by the people.

Especially important is reliable and strict control of decisions connected with the use of the armed forces. On that score there must be clear and precise constitutional guidelines. The foreign policy of the Soviet Union that made it possible to conclude the Geneva accords on Afghanistan and the withdrawal of the Soviet troops from that country is in accordance with the spirit and objective of perestroika.

The erroneous decision of moving the troops to Afghanistan must not cast any aspersions on the soldiers and officers who took part in the war. True to their oath of allegiance and convinced that they were defending the interests of the USSR and giving friendly aid to the Afghan people, they fulfilled their international duty. The Soviet people lost thousands of their sons in Afghanistan. Our sacred duty today is to hold them in remembrance as true sons of the country.

Appendix D

SUPREME SOVIET DECREE

———————

That document adopted by the Supreme Soviet acquired the force of law in the Decree of the Congress of the People's Deputies. We cite it in full.

DECREE OF THE SUPREME SOVIET, USSR

ON POLITICAL ASSESSMENT OF THE DECISION TO SEND
SOVIET TROOPS TO AFGHANISTAN IN DECEMBER 1979

1. The Congress of People's Deputies of the USSR supports the political assessment made by the Committee of the Supreme Soviet of the USSR for International Affairs on the decision to send Soviet troops to Afghanistan in 1979 and holds that that decision deserves moral and political condemnation.

2. The Congress charges the Constitutional Commission when preparing the draft of the new Constitution of the USSR to take into account the proposal aimed at finalizing the primary principles on the adoption of decisions on the use of contingents of the armed forces of the USSR, provided by paragraphs 13 and

14 of clause 113 and by paragraph 13 of clause 119 of the Constitution of the USSR currently in force, in coordination with the formulation of regulations for the Council of Defense of the USSR.

3. The Supreme Soviet of the USSR is to consider the question of setting up a commission to consider cases of former servicemen who were members of the contingent of the Soviet troops sent to Afghanistan.

4. The Council of Ministers of the USSR is charged with the formulation of a national program aimed at settling questions connected with organizing working and living conditions of former servicemen and other persons who were in the contingent of Soviet troops in Afghanistan, and also of families of deceased soldiers.

Chairman of the Supreme Soviet
of the USSR
M. Gorbachev
Moscow, the Kremlin, December 24, 1989

RECENT DEVELOPMENTS

Lately, as a result of this decree, in the Soviet Union, a number of privileges for the "Afgantsi" have been granted for housing and higher disability pensions for invalids. A special program has been drawn up, with a separate expenditure item on treatment of invalids to provide them with prosthetic appliances and wheelchairs. Assignments for treatment are obtained from military registration and enlistment offices at their places of residence and by social security offices.

Treatment is provided in several hospitals and rehabilitation centers. For example, in the Rus' hospital near Moscow they fit prosthetic appliances for lower extremities for thirty to forty persons per month. For this, they use semifinished products received from Germany. In the Crimea they are providing rehabilitation treatment at the Saki military hospital, in which a special section was set up for the treatment of "Afghan" soldiers. More than 300 men each year are receiving necessary treatment there.

A joint venture called Vosprotezprom has been set up, with special research enterprises that manufacture individual prosthetic appliances and wheelchairs.

Important work in this direction is being carried out by the Union of Veterans of Afghanistan. Last year they bought 915 wheelchairs, and fifteen men were fitted with prosthetic appliances abroad. In Moscow on Volgograd Prospect the War Invalids Hospital was furnished with imported equipment in the amount of 100,000 foreign-currency rubles. One-third of the beds in that hospital are allocated to the "Afgans." Its psychological service has provided assistance in mental rehabilitation worth 175,000 rubles. In the Central Institute of Traumatology and Orthopedics, an orthopedic clinic was established.

In another excellent program, the Union of Veterans of Afghanistan has purchased ten thermoblock plants for the construction of dwellings. The houses produced are assigned to veterans in all regions of the country.

In Moscow a Council of Mothers and Widows of Soldiers Killed in Afghanistan is headed by Roza Lysenko, whose son, a helicopter pilot, was killed in that country. The main guidelines of their activities are:

- perpetuation of the memory of sons and husbands killed in Afghanistan;
- assistance to improve conditions of life, job placement, medical service, and assistance to mothers and widows;
- assistance in repatriation of prisoners of war;
- cooperation with Soviet and foreign public organizations in the struggle for peace in the world.

Appendix E

SUMMARY OF NAJIBULLAH SPEECH

———————

THIS SPEECH OF M. NAJIBULLAH WAS GIVEN AT THE MEETING
OF THE SUPREME EXTRAORDINARY COMMISSION FOR
NATIONAL RECONCILIATION.

In the name of God merciful and all-gracious!

Noble members of the Extraordinary Commission for National Reconciliation!

Compatriots, brother Afghans on our long-suffering earth and abroad!

On behalf of the Central Committee of the People's Democratic Party of Afghanistan, the Revolutionary Council, and government of our country, I have the honor to appeal to all of you to start negotiations on national reconciliation.

By taking such a serious and important step, the party and the government are guided by the highest ideals, the interests of the people of both the present and future generations. It is only concern for the well-being of the people and for the preservation of life, in the literal sense, on Afghan soil that forms the basis of this historic initiative.

We proceed from the bitter and the instructive experience learned over the past years, from the necessity to ensure normal calm and safe conditions of life for the people now and in the future. The war has lasted in our land for almost eight years. During that time tens and hundreds of thousands of people were killed, wounded, and crippled. Enormous damage has been done to our economy, our culture, and our people.

The people are tired of the war, of endless fright, of excessive burdens and privations, of grief and tears. Families bury first one and then another dear relative.

For centuries, man has dreamed about three simple things: a place to live, good clothing, and something to eat. And what does the war force on him?

Instead of food, a bullet! Instead of a dwelling, a grave! Instead of clothes, a shroud!

We propose a cease-fire!

We propose armistice!

We propose peace!

I would like to appeal to you, citizens, to you, brother Afghan!

To you, peasant: What do you have from the war? Poverty. Extortion, threats, and intimidation. Shots at night. Think and reply to the main question: Do you need the war?

We propose peace!

I appeal to you, artisan, to you, worker: What do you have from the war? A bomb exploded in your workshop, robbers who carried away the fruits of your many years' labor. Illiterate children. Think and reply to the main question: Do you need the war?

We propose peace!

I appeal to you, merchant, to you, gray-bearded elder: What do you have from the war? Ransacked caravans with merchandise. A blown-up shop. Robbers, at night, taking away all that you earned in the daytime. Think and reply to the main question: Do you need the war?

We propose peace!

I appeal to you, honorable mullah, to you, gray-bearded elder: What do you have from the war? Demolished mosques, defiled sacred objects. Sons and daughters driven to Pakistan. Jeering at your old age. Think and reply to the main question: Do you need the war?

We propose peace!

Father, tell me: Do you need the war?

Mother, tell me: Do you need the war?

Children, tell me: Do you need the war?

Mountains and valleys, fields and gardens, tell me: Do you need the war?

I hear your voice: No, we do not need the war! All of us are fruits and branches of one tree. We need peace!

I appeal to Afghans, to every Afghan family: What do you have from the war? Deaths and funerals. Hunger. Ravaged hearths. Wanderings in search of a roof. People, think and reply to the main question: Do you need the war?

We propose peace!

I appeal to all Afghan people: Brothers, support the noble cause of peace! This appeal was born in our hearts. Let us achieve peace for the motherland, for us, for our children!

I appeal to noble ulemas and pious clergy: How long will Moslem blood be shed? Peace—it is God's precept. The great sage the Koran says: "And if two detachments of believers are fighting, reconcile them!" In an other passage it is written: "But Allah reconciled: He knows what is in one's breast, you see!" In the breast, in the hearts of our people there is only one wish today—PEACE! That is why on behalf of a long-suffering people, we wish peace, propose peace, demand peace!

I appeal to every Afghan home with simple and clear words: Peace to every home, peace to Afghanistan!

Let guns fall silent forever!

And let Allah help us!

January 3, 1987
Kabul

Appendix F

Soviet Casualties in the Afghan War
1979-1989

	Combat Losses*		Noncombat Losses		Total Losses	
	Officer	Other	Officer	Other	Officer	Other
1979	9	61	1	15	10	76
1980	170	1059	29	226	199	1285
1981	155	878	34	231	189	1109
1982	215	1408	23	302	238	1710
1983	179	878	31	358	210	1236
1984	285	1775	20	263	305	2038
1985	240	1312	33	283	273	1595
1986	198	870	18	247	216	1117
1987	189	815	23	188	212	1003
1988	53	586	64	56	117	642
1989	9	37	1	6	10	43
Totals	1702	9679	277	2175	1979	11854
%s	15	85	11	89	14	86

*Among those killed were 180 advisors and translators. Also included are those who died from wounds or disease contracted in Afghanistan between 1979 and 1989. Not included are war veterans who died from wounds or disease after 1989 or those reported missing in action.

INDEX

189